CREATIVE
POCKET HANDBOOK OF
CHRISTIAN
TRUTH

THE BIBLE ✦ GOD ✦ JESUS CHRIST

THE HOLY SPIRIT ✦ MAN ✦ SALVATION

THE CHRISTIAN ✦ CHURCH ✦ THE FUTURE

RICHARD BEWES   ROBERT F. HICKS

COMBINED VOLUME:

Authors: Richard Bewes, Robert Hicks
Design: Roger Chouler, Fred Apps, Robert Hicks
Photography: Robert Gainer Hunt, Paul Marsh, Gordon Gray, Peter Hyde
© Creative Publishing 1981
6 Pembroke Road, Moor Park, Northwood, Middlesex HA6 2HR England

This edition 1984
ISBN 1 85081 073 7

Biblical quotations taken from the New International Version of the Bible
© UK 1979 by the New York International Bible Society and used by permission.

Printed in Italy by New Interlitho S.p.A., Milan

INTRODUCTION

I commend this handbook with enthusiasm. Great trouble has been taken over its production. It contains accurate information, which is presented in a balanced and readable form. It should help large numbers of Christians all over the world to know their Bibles better, and so to know their Lord better. Bible readers of all ages will benefit from it, as it stimulates us to a deeper personal study of the great Christian fundamentals.

But these studies are not designed only for the benefit of individual readers; I am persuaded that they will equally assist busy preachers to plan their teaching programmes. They could also be of great benefit in the group studies which are springing up in their thousands across many countries, within fellowships and churches of every kind and tradition. The questions at the conclusion of each section offer a helpful basis for group discussion, and leaders are encouraged to add further questions of their own.

One of the major needs of the Christian church in every century is that its members will have a firm, intelligent faith. Too often we become victims of extremes, and find ourselves divided between arid intellectualism and unbridled emotionalism, between form and freedom, between the conservative and the radical. May this handbook help Christians everywhere – beginners and experienced alike – to lay hold personally on God's mighty revelation, which culminated in the coming of his unique Son, our Saviour, Jesus Christ.

JOHN R. W. STOTT

FOREWORD

Dear Reader,

The fact that you have obtained this handbook of Christian truth indicates your desire to understand the Bible, God's word. We are extremely glad about this. We have put this book together with the specific aim of helping our reading friends everywhere – both convinced Christians and thoughtful enquirers – to recognise some of the great landmarks in the teaching of the Bible.

When people first encounter the Bible it looks a big book, it feels an old book and – to many – it remains a closed book. But, in reality, the Bible is more than a book. *It is a library of books*, comprising God's thrilling revelation to mankind, and proving relevant in the lives of modern men and women who explore its pages.

The Bible is actually more than a single library. *It is two libraries*. The Old Testament books provide the essential background and soil from which sprang the New Testament gospel of our Lord Jesus Christ and the birth of the Christian church. How do these two libraries relate? What common theme unites them? What basic teaching do they convey?

It is our great desire that you will find this handbook to be of real value as your companion to the Bible. We shall be looking in a systematic way at the major areas of truth which convey God's revelation to mankind. These themes are the Bible itself, God, Jesus Christ, the Holy Spirit, Man, Salvation, the Christian, the Church and the Last Things.

Thus you will find in this volume nine main divisions. In all, these cover fifty-four studies, with over 300 sub-divisions. We have also provided a basic concordance (Bible Check) of over

700 key Bible passages and references. Each study is introduced with a *Key Truth*, which gives the concise emphasis of the study. After the study material, there is a *Postscript*, which draws the readers' attention to an important piece of teaching. To stimulate further thought, four questions follow, which relate to the study and may be used by individuals and groups.

By reading through these nine major areas of Bible Truth, the reader will have broadly covered the ground of God's revelation to men. The purpose of this handbook is to encourage those who sincerely want to explore this revelation for themselves. The Bible is the world's number one best-seller. But it is still an unexplored book to countless millions in spite of the many commendable new translations and paraphrases available. It is the hope and prayer of all those involved in producing this handbook that our contribution will go some way towards remedying that situation.

RICHARD BEWES
ROBERT HICKS

It is almost impossible to exaggerate the importance of studying the great truths of the Bible. I warmly commend this manual of teaching by Richard Bewes and Bob Hicks – it will meet a great need and give clear insight into the Bible's teaching.

It is my prayerful hope that these studies will introduce thousands of new believers to the thrill of discovering what the Bible says, and that they will send many of us older Christians back to our Bibles with a renewed vision for its truth.

BILLY GRAHAM

HOW TO USE THIS BOOK

Used rightly, this handbook should give years of valuable service in a number of ways. The material has been arranged for the maximum flexibility of use, and for a wide range of situations and readers.

USE IT IN PERSONAL STUDY

This handbook is a companion to the Bible. It may be used as a reference book to the teaching of the Bible, but it may also be used for personal, regular study of the scriptures. The book is made up of fifty-four studies, and if one main section is studied each week, the total material will be covered in the course of a year.

By using a good reference Bible or concordance, each study may be extended. The passages given in the Bible Check can serve as a starting point for the reader to do his own discovering in the Bible. In this way a comprehensive view of each theme can be built up. It would be useful for you to have your own notebook alongside the handbook.

USE IT IN A GROUP

The material in this handbook will be of particular value in the ever-increasing number of housegroups, where Christian people meet together. Study groups of all ages will greatly profit from the teaching they will discover for themselves as they follow the guidelines given in the book. It will also prove beneficial to women's groups, especially where newcomers to the Christian faith are eager to learn the fundamentals of their belief.

We would encourage group leaders to make the following preparations before using the handbook in any discussion. First, they should become familiar with the Bible passages provided, and be prepared to support these with cross-references. Second, they should carefully read through the study material itself. Third, they should be prepared to use the questions as a basis for discussion, and to prepare further questions of their own.

USE IT IN A CHURCH PROGRAMME
Ministers, pastors and teachers will find this handbook an invaluable reference manual for subject material when preparing programmes for the church. The material could be used by taking, for example, the six studies on Jesus Christ, using them as the basis for a six-week course of Sunday sermons or mid-week meetings.

The headings throughout the book have been so phrased that the truth of the Bible is contained within the actual words of the headings themselves. It is hoped that this will be helpful to preachers and teachers alike.

USE IT IN SCHOOLS AND COLLEGES
The teaching matter, scripture passages and questions will help to stimulate those involved in religious education, as well as members of informal religious discussion groups and forums. The handbook has been planned as a comprehensive aid so that students from many different backgrounds of worship and tradition may learn together from the Bible's teaching in a way that prepares for life.

THE BIBLE

ITS MAIN SECTIONS

The Old Testament
History
Poetry and Wisdom
Prophecy

The New Testament
History
Letters
Prophecy

ITS INSPIRATION
The identity of its divine author
The diversity of its human writers
The unity of its many themes
The authority of its inspired truth
The reality of its moral impact

ITS INTERPRETATION
Seen in its historical setting
Consistent with its surrounding passage
In harmony with the rest of scripture
Consistent with the purpose of God's revelation
Understood in changing cultures

ITS APPLICATION
Read prayerfully
Listen personally
Look expectantly
Apply regularly
Act obediently
Read totally

ITS CENTRAL THEME
The continual conflict
The promised saviour
The work of Christ
The new community
The ultimate victory

ITS CONTENTS
The Old Testament
The New Testament

GOD

THE CREATOR
God the creator
God the sustainer
God is achieving his purpose
Earth as a focal point

GOD'S BEING
God is everywhere (omnipresent)
God is all-powerful (omnipotent)
God knows everything (omniscient)
God is above space and time (eternal and unchanging)

GOD'S CHARACTER
God's truth is inseparable from his character
God's holiness reacts against all impurity
God's love extends to all mankind
God's mercy holds back what we deserve
God's grace gives us what we do not deserve
God's faithfulness provides for daily life

THE FATHERHOOD OF GOD
By creation – of all things
By covenant – of Israel
By adoption – of Christian believers
From eternity – of Jesus Christ

GOD'S REVELATION
Supremely in Jesus
Through the Bible
Through creation
In history
In man
Through human experience

THE TRINITY
Assumed in the Old Testament
Asserted in the New Testament
Accepted by faith
God the Father
God the Son
God the Holy Spirit

JESUS CHRIST

HIS INCARNATION
Christ was Son of God before time and space
It was by a supernatural conception
It upholds Christ's full deity
It establishes Christ's full humanity
It explains Christ's unique personality
It validates Christ's saving ministry

MAIN EVENTS IN THE GOSPELS
His humble birth
His sinless baptism
His prolonged temptation
His revealing transfiguration
His obedient death
His victorious resurrection
His glorious ascension

MAIN ASPECTS OF HIS MINISTRY
Authority that convinced
Parables that provoked
Miracles that confirmed
Compassion that attracted
Training the prepared
Controversy that challenged

HIS NAMES
Son of God; The Word;
High Priest; Messiah; Son of Man; Lord

HIS ATONING DEATH
Initiated a new relationship
Fulfilled Old Testament scripture
Destroyed Satan's kingdom
Reversed sin's dominion
Provided a way of victory
Guaranteed an eternity with God

HIS TRIUMPHANT RESURRECTION
The foundation of the Christian faith
An event supported by evidence
A promise of ultimate victory
The power of Christian experience
The assurance of eternal security

HOLY SPIRIT

HIS PERSON
He is the third person of the Trinity
He knows as a person (mind)
He feels as a person (emotion)
He acts as a person (will)

HIS NAMES AND DESCRIPTIONS
The Holy Spirit
The Spirit of God
The Spirit of Christ
The Spirit of Truth
The Counsellor or Helper
Wind; Water; Fire; Oil; Dove

HIS WORK
He convinces of sin
He illuminates truth
He reveals Christ
He lives in believers
He inspires prayer
He prepares for heaven

HIS ACTIVITY IN THE CHRISTIAN
Life – new birth by the Spirit
Assurance – the witness of the Spirit
Unity – fellowship in the Spirit
Ownership – the seal of the Spirit
Power – the fullness of the Spirit
Confidence – the pledge of the Spirit

HIS FRUIT
Love; Joy; Peace; Patience; Kindness; Goodness;
Faithfulness; Gentleness; Self-control

HIS GIFTS
The gifts exalt Christ
The gifts involve all
The gifts should unite all
Gifts lay foundations
Gifts build up the fellowship
Gifts promote mission

MAN

HIS UNIQUENESS
A whole being, physical and spiritual
A spiritual being, made in God's image
A personal being, with mind, emotion and will
A moral being, responsible for his actions

HIS DIVERSITY
Natural dimensions
Creative dimension
Cultural dimensions
Social dimensions
Religious dimensions

HIS REBELLION AND FALL
Man's innocence gave him fellowship with God
Man's freedom gave him the power of choice
Man's choice gave him true responsibility
Man's decision led him into moral rebellion

HIS REBELLION AND CONDEMNATION
Rebellion and guilt
Guilt and condemnation
Condemnation and separation
Separation and death

HIS QUEST AND DILEMMA
His religious search
His philosophical wanderings
His psychological contradictions
His physical drive

HIS ENEMIES
Satan; Sin; The world; The flesh; Death.

SALVATION

GOD'S PLAN FOR MANKIND
God's plan – his will is sovereign
God's plan – his work is eternal
God's plan – his choice is specific
God's people – separated for holy living
God's people – called to good works
God's people – preparing for future glory

MAN'S NEED OF SALVATION
Man's need of a new direction
Man's need of a new nature
Man's need of a new motivation
Man's need of personal fulfilment
Man's need of social acceptance
Man's need of a spiritual direction

THE WAY OF SALVATION
The basis – the death of Jesus
The basis – the resurrection of Jesus
The call – to repentance
The call – to faith
The promise – forgiveness
The promise – the gift of the Spirit

ACCEPTANCE
God regenerates the believer as a new being
God reconciles the believer in a new relationship
God redeems the believer through a new covenant
God justifies the believer for a new position
God glorifies the believer for a new life

SANCTIFICATION
A separation to God
A separation from the world
A separation for holy living
A separation by the Holy Spirit
A separation through the word of God
A separation that progresses throughout life

IN THE LETTER TO THE ROMANS
Condemnation; Justification; Reconciliation;
Identification; Liberation; Sanctification; Election;
Transformation

THE CHRISTIAN

DESCRIBED
A sinner saved by grace
A member of God's family
A disciple of Jesus Christ
A temple of the Holy Spirit
A pilgrim in an alien environment
A citizen of heaven

THE CHRISTIAN AND THE BIBLE
Directs the Christian for life
Equips the Christian for battle
Energises the Christian for service
Corrects the Christian from error
Develops the Christian in the faith
Informs the Christian of God's mind

THE CHRISTIAN AND PRAYER
For communion with God
For growth in God
For the service of God
For the praise of God
For the experience of God

THE CHRISTIAN AND WITNESS
Proclaiming a person
Explaining the truth; Sharing a love
Witnessing consistently, personally,
collectively

THE CHRISTIAN AND THE WORLD
Called out of the world
Separated from the world
Sent into the world
To overcome the world
To journey through the world

THE CHRISTIAN LIFE
A vocation to be fulfilled
A character to be developed
A fellowship to be maintained
Energies to be harnessed
Minds to be developed
A hope to be realised

THE CHURCH

ITS CHARACTERISTICS
It is the church of Jesus Christ (historical)
It is the company of all believers (universal)
It is a unity of the Spirit (spiritual)
Its authority is God's word (scriptural)
Its programme is world-wide (international)
Its destiny is heaven (eternal)

ITS MAIN DESCRIPTION
A firm building; A virgin bride; A functioning body;
A permanent city; A stable family; An active army

ITS RELATIONSHIP TO CHRIST
Christ died for the church
Christ builds the church
Christ protects the church
Christ purifies the church
Christ intercedes for the church
Christ prepares for the church

ITS AUTHORITY AND MISSION
Guarding the truth; Correcting the unruly;
Challenging evil; Evangelising the world;
Serving the world; Glorifying God

ITS ORDINANCES
Baptism
Admission to membership
More than a symbol
Death to the old life
Rising to the new life
Identification with Christ

The Lord's Supper
We commemorate; We communicate;
We appropriate; We participate;
We anticipate

ITS MINISTRY AND ORDER
Preaching and teaching
Prayer and intercession
Fellowship and caring
Worship and praise
Leadership and government

THE FUTURE

THE HOPE OF THE CHRISTIAN
The promise to God's people
The fulfilment of God's purposes
The defeat of God's enemies
A living hope
A steadfast hope
A purifying hope

THE PRELUDE TO CHRIST'S RETURN
In the natural realm
In the social realm
In the international realm
In the family realm
In the personal realm
In the spiritual realm

THE RETURN OF CHRIST
Prophetically; Personally;
Visibly; Suddenly; Triumphantly; Conclusively

THE JUDGEMENT
God will be declared as just
Christ will be acknowledged as Lord
Christians will be accountable for their service
The disobedient will be rejected for their unbelief
Satan will be destroyed for ever

THE RESURRECTION
Christ its guarantee
Nature its illustration
Eternal life its outcome
From humiliation to glory
From the natural to the spiritual
From mortality to immortality

THE NEW ORDER
The triumph of the Lamb
The new creation
The new Jerusalem
Paradise restored
Jesus is coming

The Bible

ITS MAIN SECTIONS

The Key Truth   *There are 66 books in the Bible, collected in two 'libraries'. They were written over a period of some 1,500 years. These books can be placed in the following sections:*

THE OLD TESTAMENT
History

The historical books of the Old Testament (from Genesis to Esther) show how God is involved in human history. He created the world, he chose a people to carry out his plan for saving all mankind and he provided them with laws for correct living.

These books of the law and the story of the nation of Israel provide the foundation for New Testament Christianity.

Poetry and Wisdom

Proverbs, riddles, songs, parables and allegories all occur in the wisdom and poetry books (from Job to the Song of Solomon). These books mirror the human response to God and to life. Despair, love and joy; the emptiness of life without God; bitter anger and triumphant faith – every emotion and situation has purpose when God is in the picture.

Prophecy

The prophets were men whom God called to speak for him to his people. They explained the **past**, reminding the people of God's law and his promises; they challenged the evils of the **present**; they also declared the **future** acts of God. Although these 17 books often speak of judgement and doom, they also tell of a future hope – the coming of a Messiah and of a new relationship with God.

BIBLE CHECK

History Genesis 12:1-3   Joshua 24:14,15
Poetry and Wisdom   Psalm 127   Ecclesiastes 3:1-9

THE NEW TESTAMENT

History

The four Gospels are based on the accounts of eye-witnesses who heard and saw Jesus of Nazareth, and they identify him as the Messiah, in fulfilment of the Old Testament.

The book of Acts goes on to show what took place after the death and resurrection of Jesus, and how the Christian church grew within the Jewish and Gentile worlds.

Letters

The New Testament letters were addressed to individuals, churches or groups of churches. They give the reader a vivid impression of the life of the first Christians, and the problems they faced.

These letters often show us the mistakes that Christians made, alongside the teaching of the apostles that gave correction and guidance in Christian living. Because Christians still have similar needs and weaknesses, the 21 New Testament letters have relevance for the church in every age.

Prophecy

The final book in the Bible consists of a series of visions seen by the apostle John, which reveal the situation affecting believers, unbelievers and the whole created order.

The book of Revelation is written in the language of symbolism and prophecy. It has inspired Christians down the ages with its message of the God who controls history, and who finally defeats all the powers of evil.

Postscript   *One of the remarkable things about the Bible is that although it is a very old book, written to guide people in their lives centuries ago, it is still able to answer the needs of people today.*

Prophecy   Amos 5:21-24   Isaiah 53
History   Mark 1:14,15   John 20:30,31   Acts 1:1-3
Letters   Romans 12:1,2   Titus 3:3-8   1 Peter 2:9
Prophecy   Revelation 1:8-11; 12:7-12; 22:12,13

THOUGHT STARTERS

1 Read Luke 24:13-35. What does this tell us about the Bible's power to banish fear and aid understanding? Notice the number of sections in the Old Testament referred to in verses 27 and 44.

2 While all scripture is inspired by God, some books may be of more immediate importance than others. Which do you think these are, from both the Old and New Testaments?

3 Look at 2 Timothy 3:16,17. Why has God given us the Bible?

4 Look at Galatians 3:29. What does this teach us about the relationship of the Old Testament to the New?

Alpine meadow, Bernese Oberland in Switzerland. 'In the past God spoke to our forefathers through the prophets . . .' (Hebrews 1:1).

ITS INSPIRATION

The Key Truth *When we say that the Bible is 'inspired' we mean that God spoke his message through the people that he chose. These people did not become like robots under God's control, but kept their own identities, while being guided by God.*

The identity of its divine author

The Bible claims that God is its ultimate author. The conviction that God was speaking through the messages of the Old Testament is expressed many hundreds of times.

Both the Jewish people and the New Testament writers accepted that the Old Testament was inspired by God. Jesus himself upheld this view. He believed the scriptures, and by the way he quoted them showed that they were more important than human opinions and traditions.

The New Testament writers, for their part, were also aware that they were not teaching human wisdom, but rather God's message to men.

The diversity of its human writers

The biblical writers came from many different cultures and eras and represented a very wide range of intellects and abilities.

There was a diversity of circumstance. Some wrote as prisoners in exile, while others ruled kingdoms. There was a diversity of employment. Some were ordinary bakers, shepherds or tent-makers, while others enjoyed high positions in society. There was a diversity of character – from the despairing to the joyful.

BIBLE CHECK

Divine Author   Jeremiah 1:9   2 Peter 1:21   2 Timothy 3:16,17
Human Writers   Amos 7:14,15   1 Kings 4:29-32   Acts 18:3

The unity of its many themes

This unique library of books confronts the reader with its unity, although written over some 1,500 years. It is ancient, yet modern in its relevance to human needs. It is diverse, yet one – held together by its common theme of God's people and their desire and need of a coming Saviour. The Old Testament finds its fulfilment in the New Testament. The New Testament has its roots in the Old Testament. The library is one.

The authority of its inspired truth

From early times the value of these books so impressed themselves on God's people that they acknowledged their authority and received them into the category of inspired scripture. They recognised that it was God who was speaking.

It was not the act of binding the books into the Bible that gave them their inspiration. *This they already possessed.* The authority of the Old Testament was recognised by the Jews, by Jesus himself, and also by the New Testament writers, who frequently quoted the Old Testament. The New Testament writings were also accepted by the church from its early days as having the final say in everything that Christians believe and do.

The reality of its moral impact

The Bible is not afraid to portray evil honestly, even when some of its finest characters are involved in it. But in contrast, it also shows us the highest moral standard in history – the life of Jesus Christ.

This is the book that consistently challenges evil, transforms lives and exalts Christ.

Postscript *Like any other book, the Bible was written by men. But, unlike any other book, it was guided and planned by God from beginning to end. It is because God stands behind the Bible that all Christians owe it their loyalty and their obedience to its demands.*

Its Unity Matthew 5:17,18 Luke 24:25-27,44
Its Authority Joshua 1:7,8 Matthew 22:29 Psalm 19:7-11
Moral Impact Deuteronomy 32:45-47 Hebrews 4:12

THOUGHT STARTERS

1 Read Exodus 3:1-14 and 4:1-17. Why was Moses reluctant to speak for God? What reasons did God give for trusting him?

2 When the prophets spoke God's message they were often attacked or even killed by the people. Why? Does this still happen today?

3 How did Jesus regard the scriptures? See Matthew 5:17-19. How can we best learn from his example?

4 God spoke through the writers of the Bible without robbing them of their individuality. Consider some of these writers. What do we learn from this about the way in which God uses people?

Sunset over a fiord, Norway. 'All Scripture is God-breathed'
(2 Timothy 3:16).

ITS INTERPRETATION

The Key Truth *Interpretation means the discovery of the true meaning of the Bible. Several things are important to remember as we try to understand the Bible's teaching.*

IT MUST BE –

Seen in its historical setting

One of the ways in which we can understand the meaning of a Bible passage is to gain an understanding of its *original* meaning to the earliest readers. The more we know about the customs and politics of Bible times, the clearer its meaning will be.

For example, the New Testament commands that slaves should obey their masters. We must understand this in light of the fact that slavery was generally accepted at that time (even though it was seen as part of the order that was passing away because of Christ).

Similarly, a knowledge of customs at that time helps the modern reader to understand the meaning of Jesus' command to his disciples to wash one another's feet – which might otherwise seem irrelevant today.

Consistent with its surrounding passage

We can better understand the meaning of a Bible word when we examine the sentence in which it occurs. In the same way, we can only truly understand a sentence when we look at the surrounding paragraph.

The leaders of many false cults and sects often twist the truth of the Bible by taking a sentence out of its context. In this way they use the Bible to support their own beliefs. Christians must be careful to find out what the Bible is really saying – even when it hurts.

BIBLE CHECK

Historical Setting Ephesians 6:5 John 13:14
Surrounding Passage Nehemiah 8:8 2 Corinthians 4:2

In harmony with the rest of scripture

Individual passages of scripture are to be interpreted in the light of the whole Bible. When this is done, no one part of scripture will be found to conflict with another. When we are confronted with apparent contradictions in the Bible, it is probably because we do not know the consistent teaching of the Bible as a whole.

The challenge to the reader of the Bible is to develop a truly biblical way of thinking.

Consistent with the purpose of God's revelation

The Bible tells us all that we need to know about God's plan for his creation and for mankind. There are many questions which we might want answered, about which the Bible says very little or nothing. But God's word tells us all we *need* to know about him and his plans.

We must recognise that the Bible is first of all a book of salvation. Therefore, we should avoid making clever interpretations on matters outside its main purpose.

Understood in changing cultures

The Bible has a living message, with power to transform lives and characters. Although it was given in cultures far removed from those of modern times, its relevance to life is undiminished today.

As we interpret the Bible, however, we must be prepared to wrestle with the words and terms used by the biblical writers, and to translate them in ways that the modern reader can understand.

Postscript   *The Bible is not a scientific textbook, nor a history book. Yet it will not conflict with scientific findings nor with historical facts. Its purpose is different — that of portraying God's plan for mankind, in Christ.*

Harmony   Matthew 22:29   2 Timothy 2:15
Purpose   Deuteronomy 29:29   2 Timothy 3:14,15
Cultures   Acts 8:34-38   Acts 17:11

THOUGHT STARTERS

1 Read John 13:1-15. In the time of Jesus, to wash someone's feet was an act of humility and kindness. In what ways can we obey Jesus' command in verse 14 today?

2 Some words used in the Bible are not a part of everyday speech. Find out what words like 'salvation' or 'repentance' mean, and put them in your own words.

3 What should our reaction be when we find equally Christian people divided over the correct interpretation of a Bible passage?

4 What is the strength of knowing individual verses of the Bible by heart? What is the limitation?

Reflections in Bachsee, Switzerland. 'And we, who with unveiled faces all reflect the Lords' glory, are being transformed into his likeness . . .' (2 Corinthians 3:18).

ITS APPLICATION

The Key Truth *The Bible is meant to change the way in which we live. As we apply the Bible, God instructs, supports, cleanses and directs us in our daily lives.*

Read prayerfully

The Bible is not simply an interesting book to read, it is a book to get involved in. It deals with issues that vitally concern the reader's life, character and destiny.

To read the Bible after praying is a safeguard against hardness or pride – it also shows that the reader is willing to submit to God's moral direction.

Listen personally

The Bible is not a book of abstract philosophy – it is a book about life and about people in real situations. Isaiah spoke specifically to the people of Jerusalem. The apostle Paul often greeted friends by name in his letters. The book of Revelation was written to Christians who were suffering persecution.

But we must go on to say that the Bible's rewards and promises are for every reader, of whatever century. As we open our lives to the Bible's message, we can expect God to communicate with us.

Look expectantly

As we read the Bible, we will be surprised and even shocked by some of the events that act as warnings within its pages. There will be other passages that challenge or puzzle us. We must expect to be stretched to the limit of our capacity by this book.

BIBLE CHECK

Prayerfully Psalm 119:33-40 Matthew 7:7,8
Personally 1 Samuel 3:10 Revelation 1:3

Apply regularly

When we read and apply the Bible regularly, one of the great benefits is that we start to see the world in a Christian way. We also see the Bible as a whole, and not as unconnected fragments.

As young children need a regular diet for proper growth, so the Christian needs to feed spiritually upon the scriptures, applying their truths to daily living. As a result, our characters are transformed.

Act obediently

The Christian will repeatedly be confronted with the Bible's commands. The Bible challenges us to obey God's word, and not only to listen to it.

Jesus said that it is not enough merely to hear his words. It is only when we hear *and obey* that our lives are like a house built on rock – safe and secure.

Read totally

The Bible reader should aim at a full and balanced appreciation of all that the Bible may teach on any given topic. To rely on individual verses or on favourite selected passages (valuable though these are) will not lead us to spiritual maturity.

As we persist in reading the Bible thoroughly, worship becomes a living force, our work for God becomes a vital activity, and Christ becomes a daily companion.

Postscript   *God gave us the Bible not just for us to enjoy its stories, or learn about him. He gave us the Bible so that we may live in the way that he wants. Applying the Bible can be challenging and uncomfortable – but it must be done.*

Expectantly   Jeremiah 23:29   1 John 5:13
Regularly   Psalm 1:1,2   1 Peter 2:2,3
Obediently   James 1:22-25   Matthew 7:24-27
Totally   2 Corinthians 4:2   Colossians 3:16

THOUGHT STARTERS

1 Read Psalm 119:97-112. Try to list some of the benefits that result from meditating on the scriptures.

2 Christ once told a parable about the different kinds of soil into which the good seed fell (Mark 4:1-20). Try to describe the kind of life that is 'good soil', in which the seed of God's word can grow.

3 Discuss with your friends in practical terms the times of day when you find it best to read the Bible.

4 Hebrews 4:12 describes the power of the scriptures. Try to enumerate some of the instances in the Bible where this power was demonstrated.

A group meets to study the Bible. 'The precepts of the Lord are right, giving joy to the heart' (Psalm 19:8).

ITS CENTRAL THEME

The Key Truth *Although mankind has rebelled against God and ignored his laws, God has a plan for rescuing men. This plan is centred around Jesus Christ, and concludes in God's ultimate victory over sin, Satan and death.*

The continual conflict

The conflict in the Bible began when Adam and Eve questioned God's authority. From this simple beginning stemmed the entrance of sin into the world, and the revolt of mankind against God's rule.

The Bible traces the spread of this conflict between men and God. It shows how men soon became hostile to each other, as well as to God. The need of humanity to be reconciled to God becomes the central theme of the Bible.

The promised saviour

The Old Testament speaks clearly about the longing for a future deliverer from sin and guilt. However, this is more than a mere hope. The prophets, particularly, speak of God's promise of a Saviour, who will establish a new agreement with God's people – with forgiveness and liberated service at its heart.

The New Testament points unmistakably to Jesus Christ as being this promised Saviour.

The work of Christ

The coming of Jesus Christ in history fulfils all the hopes of the Old Testament, and provides the basis for the New. In Jesus, God himself entered human history, and opened the way for forgiveness and holy living. This was done through Christ's death, his resurrection and his gift of the Spirit. Death is de-

---

BIBLE CHECK

The Conflict   Genesis 3   Titus 3:3
The Saviour   Isaiah 53   Jeremiah 31:31-34   Luke 24:44,45

feated, the power of Satan is broken, and the ascended Christ rules.

The new community

The New Testament portrays the followers of Christ as the society of the saved – called to be members of his world-wide church. Wherever the rule of Christ operates in people's lives, there his church is found.

This new community worships its reigning Lord, and is called upon to fulfil its mission of evangelism and practical service to the whole world. Jesus Christ personally upholds it in every experience. When he comes again, its membership and task will be complete.

The ultimate victory

The whole of creation will be involved in the final triumph of God. His love and justice will be upheld for everyone to see, and the whole empire of evil will be overthrown.

The great landmark of the future is the return of Jesus Christ, personally, historically, visibly and triumphantly. He will come as Judge of the whole world as well as Saviour of his people. The date of his coming cannot be predicted, although calamities, wars and the appearance of false Christs confirm the approach of this final event of history.

Christian believers look forward to a new heaven and a new earth. They look forward to a day when they will receive new bodies which will never age or die. Then sin and sorrow will be banished for ever, and their salvation will be complete.

Postscript *It is important for the Bible reader to understand, by consistently reading the whole Bible, that God is at the centre of all things, and is in ultimate control of the universe.*

Christ's Work Mark 1:15 Luke 2:28-32 Titus 3:4-7
Community Matthew 16:18; 28:19,20 Ephesians 2:18-22
Victory 1 Thessalonians 4:13-18 Revelation 21:1-4

THOUGHT STARTERS

1 Consider Titus 3: 3-7. How far are the major themes of the Bible summed up in this passage? Are Paul's words true of your own experience?

2 A Chinese person once said of the Bible, 'Whoever made this book made me.' Do you agree with this? What lies behind such a sentence?

3 What is the *most important* reason for having a biblical way of looking at life? Because the Bible brings comfort and hope? Because society needs belief of some kind? Because the Bible is true? Try to give your reasons.

4 How does a biblical view of life help a person to grapple with the issues of wrongdoing, strife and injustice?

A mountain path on Snowdon, Wales. 'He explained to them what was said in all the Scriptures concerning himself' (Luke 24:27).

ITS CONTENTS

The Key Truth *Each book of the Bible has its own distinctive central themes. Below is a sample of some of these themes:*

THE OLD TESTAMENT

Genesis: The start of God's plan for his people.
Exodus: God's people are freed from slavery.
Leviticus: Preparing God's people for worship.
Numbers: God's people wander in the wilderness.
Deuteronomy: God's people called to obedience.
Joshua: Success in the Promised Land.
Judges: Failure in the Promised Land.
Ruth: The story of a faithful daughter-in-law.
1 Samuel: The emergence of Israel as a kingdom.
2 Samuel: Israel's greatest King – David.
1 Kings: Solomon – the Temple – the division.
2 Kings: The divided kingdom, and the prophets.
1 Chronicles: God's faithfulness to his people.
2 Chronicles: The fall of Israel as a nation.
Ezra: The return from exile, and the new start.
Nehemiah: Danger as Jerusalem is rebuilt.
Esther: Esther's courage saves the exiled Jews.
Job: Dialogues on the sufferings of a godly man.
Psalms: Man's honest response to God.
Proverbs: Wisdom for living.
Ecclesiastes: The world's philosophy exposed.
Song of Solomon: A poem of love.
Isaiah: The prophet of hope.
Jeremiah: The prophet of tragedy.
Lamentations: The prophet of sorrow.
Ezekiel: The prophet of God's glory.
Daniel: The prophet of confidence in God.
Hosea: The prophet of love.
Joel: The prophet of the Day of the Lord.
Amos: The prophet of justice.
Obadiah: The prophet of doom.
Jonah: The prophet of repentance.
Micah: The prophet of restitution.

Nahum: The prophet of retribution.
Habakkuk: The prophet of doubt and faith.
Zephaniah: The prophet of judgement.
Haggai: The prophet of dedication.
Zechariah: The prophet of restoration.
Malachi: The prophet of expectation.

THE NEW TESTAMENT

Matthew: The teaching of the promised Messiah.
Mark: The work of a powerful Saviour.
Luke: The concern of a loving Saviour.
John: The belief in a personal Saviour.
Acts: The witness to a risen Saviour.
Romans: God's righteousness upheld and applied.
1 Corinthians: A church's problems corrected.
2 Corinthians: The ministry of the church.
Galatians: The gospel and Jewish law contrasted.
Ephesians: Christ's relationship with the church.
Philippians: The love and loyalty of a church.
Colossians: The person of Jesus exalted.
1 Thessalonians: New converts encouraged.
2 Thessalonians: The second coming of Christ.
1 Timothy: Instructions for church behaviour.
2 Timothy: The pastor of a church encouraged.
Titus: Christian self-control.
Philemon: To the owner of a runaway slave.
Hebrews: The greatness of Christ exalted.
James: Practical instructions for a living faith.
1 Peter: The suffering of the church explained.
2 Peter: The perils of the church foretold.
1 John: The reality of divine fellowship.
2 John: Walking in the truth exhorted.
3 John: Living in the truth practised.
Jude: Apostasy in the church condemned.
Revelation: The triumph of God over all evil.

Postscript   *Each book of the Bible should be read as a whole, so that an overall view is gained of its contribution to God's message to men.*

Please Note   *The above themes are only a guide. Each theme should not be seen as the only theme of any particular book, but as a distinct emphasis of that book.*

THOUGHT STARTERS

1 Look at Matthew 4: 1-11. Consider each of the temptations that confronted Jesus. Why did he use the Old Testament so much to resist the Devil? What may we learn from this?

2 Discuss with your friends which biblical book has helped you most, so far. How has it helped? Which book do you look forward to reading next? Why?

3 Why is it important to read the Bible? Look up 1 John 5:13 and John 20:31.

4 Perhaps you feel daunted by the thought of getting to know the books of the Bible. What is the best way of arranging your Bible-reading programme?

Flags in Vienna. 'The eternal gospel . . . to every nation, tribe, language and people' (Revelation 14:6).

God

THE CREATOR

The Key Truth *God has brought into existence the whole of creation, which he sustains and upholds by his power. He created the universe out of nothing, and did this for his own purpose and glory.*

God the creator

The universe has not always existed. The consistent teaching of scripture is that the cosmos had a beginning. It was not formed from any matter that already existed. God, the one and only creator of the universe, brought the world into being by the unaided power of his word.

God did not *need* to create the universe, for he is self-sufficient. He decided to bring all things into being for his own glory. The creation involved all three persons of the Godhead. The opening chapter of the Bible records our beginnings in majestic and timeless language that communicates to every culture and era.

God the sustainer

The Bible teaches that God the creator is also the provider and sustainer of all that he has brought into being. He is not an absentee God who made the world and then left it to run itself.

Far from remaining aloof and remote from his creation God continues to work in it. He is intimately involved in the running of the universe and the forces of nature, and he is in overall control of governments and communities. Christ also taught of the Father's concern for the least of his creatures.

BIBLE CHECK

Creator Nehemiah 9:6 Hebrews 11:3 Genesis 1
Sustainer Acts 14:17 Hebrews 1:3

God is achieving his purpose

God is in ultimate control of all that he has created. This does not mean that we are unable to decide things freely for ourselves. God has given us that freedom – even though we chose to rebel against him. But it does mean that God is active, and is bringing about the things he wants to happen. He is achieving his purpose.

God's purpose may be stated very simply. It is to restore fallen humanity and the creation itself to the freedom and perfection that have been lost because of mankind's rebellion. God the creator is also God the redeemer.

Earth as a focal point

The earth is a very small planet in a vast universe, and it could not be argued that our world occupies any central position in creation. But it is apparent from the Bible that the creator of the cosmos has set his loving concern upon this earth.

Man is physically dwarfed by the immensity of his surroundings, but the universe should hold no terrors for him, because of the place the world has in God's purpose. Ours is the visited planet, the part of creation where a special relationship has been planned between God and ourselves, who have been formed in his image. Man is central to God's plan for the whole universe.

Postscript *A person who is in rebellion against the creator will inevitably have a man-centred view of God and creation. The Christian learns to see creation as it really is, with God at the centre and in control.*

Purpose Daniel 2:20-22 Romans 8:18-25
Focal Point Psalm 8:3-9 Revelation 21:1-3

THOUGHT STARTERS

1 Read Genesis 1, and think about its description of the world's beginnings. Where does this chapter place you, as a person, in the universe? See Psalm 8:3-8.

2 The Bible gives us reasons to feel happy with ourselves as human beings, but also to feel unhappy. Why is this?

3 What features in our world do you most appreciate, and give thanks for?

4 Why is the truth of creation important today? Is it enough to say that God is the creator, or should we regard the details of *how* he created important as well?

Indian Elephant. 'God saw all that he had made, and it was very good' (Genesis 1:31).

GOD'S BEING

The Key Truth   *There are certain aspects of God's being that are unique to him, and can never be shared with any other being.*

God is everywhere (omnipresent)

God is the creator of nature, and is therefore not to be confused with it (the mistake of the *Pantheists*). At the same time we should not separate God from his creation and think of him as absent (the mistake of the *Deists*).

The Bible teaches us that there is no place in creation to which we can go that will put us at a distance from God. He is present everywhere in the universe. We must be careful not to limit God in the way that he is present among men. He is present *creatively* in his works; he is present *morally* in the area of human behaviour; he is present *spiritually* among his people; he is present sovereignly in nations, governments and systems.

God is all-powerful (omnipotent)

The Bible gives us many examples of God's power. He brings the designs of powerful nations to nothing. He is in control of nature – and this comes out especially in the miracles Jesus performed.

However, all these instances might suggest to us that God is just a lot more powerful that we are. The fact that he is *all-powerful* is shown by his role as the creator of all things, the judge of all men, and the one who will subdue all the forces of evil. The Bible tells us he is the only God, and all power belongs to him.

BIBLE CHECK

Omnipresent   Psalm 139:7-12   Jeremiah 23:23,24
Omnipotent   Genesis 17:1   Job 42:1,2   Jeremiah 32:17

God knows everything (omniscient)

God's knowledge follows from his universal presence. Because he fills heaven and earth, all things are open to his view and knowledge. He is completely aware of the past, present and future. He knows about all events, thoughts, feelings and actions.

The knowledge gained by other beings must be built up and learned. God's knowledge is eternal and is entirely his own – he has learned it from nobody.

This teaching is vital to our understanding of God. If God did not know everything, it would not be possible to believe in the justice of his judgements in history and at the end of time. This is also true in the realm of worship. The Christian prays to a God who fully understands our state and our needs, who hears and perceives not only our words but our secret thoughts and desires, and who knows the end from the beginning.

God is above space and time (eternal and unchanging)

The Bible describes God as the first and the last. He always has existed, and he owes his existence to no one. In contrast to the ever-changing and decaying world, the scriptures teach us that God is unchanging in his person and purposes.

He neither increases nor decreases. He can never be wiser, holier or more merciful than he has ever been or ever will be.

For the believer, limited by a temporary body and a changing environment, the eternal God provides a permanent foundation and a secure home and resting place.

Postscript   *These descriptions of God only give us half of the biblical picture of him. It is the moral aspect of God which completes the picture and shows us that goodness is at the heart of the universe.*

Omniscient   Psalm 139:1-6   Hebrews 4:12,13
Eternal   Isaiah 44:6   Malachi 3:6   James 1:17

THOUGHT STARTERS

1 Read Psalm 139:1-18. What major truths about God are expressed in verses 1-6, 7-12 and 13-18? How does the writer see his relationship to God? Try to list all that God has done for him.

2 How should our understanding of God's being affect the way that we pray? After thinking about this, turn to Psalm 139:23,24

3 Look at Deuteronomy 29:29. How do these words of Moses help us in matters where our knowledge (e.g. of the future) is limited?

4 Try and make the praises of the apostle Paul your own, as you worship God in the words of Romans 11:33-36.

Niagara Falls. 'The Lord . . . said, "I am God Almighty"' (Genesis 17:1).

GOD'S CHARACTER ·

The Key Truth *The truth, holiness and goodness of God find expression in his works and actions, extending even to those in rebellion against his rule.*

God's truth is inseparable from his character

The truth of God is the foundation of all knowledge. Truth is unalterable. It will not change or accommodate itself to varying cultures and standards. Truth is essential to God himself – it always has existed and always will exist.

Thus our existence is not a delusion, as some people claim, and the laws of the universe will not shift. Truth comes from God and is consistent with his character. We see this supremely in the person of Jesus who, as Son of God, claimed to be the centre of all truth.

God's holiness reacts against all impurity

God is holy. There is no statement in the Bible which is more demanding that this. God's holiness means he is totally committed to goodness and is at war with evil.

The Bible teaches that God alone is completely pure and free from evil. As a result, it is impossible for wrongdoers to live in God's presence until they have been made clean.

God's love extends to all mankind

The scriptures are full of the love, mercy, grace and faithfulness of God. Human love is seen as an imperfect reflection of the love that characterises God.

This is the love that longs to pardon the evildoer, while yet satisfying the demands of divine justice. Its highest expression is seen at the cross.

God's mercy holds back what we deserve

God's holiness and moral purity demand that those

BIBLE CHECK

Truth Jeremiah 14:14 Numbers 23:19 John 14:6
Holiness Isaiah 6:1-5 Habakkuk 1:13 Revelation 15:4
Love Psalm 103:13 John 3:16 1 John 4:7-11

who revolt against his authority should face judgement and be overthrown. However, the Bible is full of examples of the restraining hand of God's mercy.

Thus the Bible shows us that God is slow to punish sin. He prefers to give people the opportunity to turn from wrong.

God's grace gives us what we do not deserve

The word 'grace' means that 'God is generous towards us even though we deserve his anger'. There are two kinds of grace. On one level there is *common grace*, where God's gifts in nature (the seasons, our natural abilities and human relationships) are given to the human race, regardless of the attitude of those who receive.

On a spiritual level, we receive God's *saving grace*. He has given his assurances and promises to mankind throughout history, sending his messengers to raise the standards of societies and to free them from slavery to evil. Supremely, he has given his Son to the world, so that the gift of eternal life might be freely available – to those who respond.

God's faithfulness provides for daily life

The writers of the Psalms constantly refer to the faithfulness of God, illustrated in the ceaseless cycle of nature and in the return of the morning each day. It is God's world, and his resources are around us.

Man has to face danger and hardship in a world which is imperfect because of the intrusion of sin – and the Christian is as liable to face illness and testing as the non-Christian. But those with a trust in God are assured of his overall care and control of events.

Postscript   *It is important to see all the aspects of God's character. If we only see God as holy, he will appear harsh and demanding. If we only see him as loving, he will seem to be unjust and powerless.*

Mercy   Nehemiah 9:16,17   Hosea 11:8,9   2 Peter 3:9
Grace   Matthew 5:43-45   1 Corinthians 1:4-8   Ephesians 2:8-10
Faithfulness   Psalm 89:1,2   1 Thessalonians 5:23,24

THOUGHT STARTERS

1 Consider the teaching of Psalm 103, and try to list some of the qualities of God's character that are featured there. Which of these qualities have you felt to be at work in your own life?

2 What is the biblical answer to those of us who carry on sinning, taking it for granted that God will forgive us? Consider your reply in the light of Romans 2:4,5.

3 What is the difference between God's *common grace* and his *saving grace*? Who are the receivers of God's gifts in each case?

4 How can we best express our gratitude to God for the goodness that we have received from him?

Gwynedd, North Wales. 'Whenever . . . the rainbow appears I will remember my covenant . . . Never again will the waters become a flood to destroy all life' (Genesis 9:14).

THE FATHERHOOD OF GOD

The Key Truth   *God is Father, generally, of the creation he has made. He is also Father to all Christians, whom he has adopted into his family. But uniquely, he is the Father of Jesus Christ.*

By creation – of all things

Although the Bible never designates God directly as 'Father of the creation', nevertheless his creativity is frequently linked with his character as Father. The universe is under his care and fatherly authority.

In the scriptures, God is portrayed as Father of mankind only in a general sense – because he created us. The close and intimate relationship that could exist between God and the individual believer was not fully revealed until it was taught and made possible by Jesus Christ. God is the Father of all people, but only in a very limited sense. This is because of the universal rebellion against God's authority that has characterised the human race throughout history.

By covenant – of Israel

In the Old Testament, God initiated a solemn agreement with Israel, by which he would be their God, and the people of Israel would be his people, and would submit to his rule and authority.

It was in this national sense that God became the Father of Israel, giving to his people guidance, protection – and discipline on the many occasions when he was disobeyed.

BIBLE CHECK

By Creation   Acts 17:24-29   Ephesians 4:6
By Covenant   Isaiah 63:16   Malachi 2:10

By adoption – of Christian believers

It was Jesus Christ who revealed the fatherhood of God towards believers in an intimate sense unknown in any other faith. He taught his followers to speak to God as their heavenly Father.

As the New Testament teaching develops, we learn that salvation includes, first, giving the new believer forgiveness and the right to stand before God. But secondly, we are adopted into the circle of God's family, with all the privileges that follow. Thirdly and better still, we are given the *spirit* of sonship, and a change of heart that encourages us to speak to God as a child would to its own father.

Such a relationship knows no human parallel. Those who have entered into such a relationship can truly be said to have been born of God. They are his children.

From eternity – of Jesus Christ

It is true that Jesus addressed God in his prayers as 'Father', but he never joined in prayer with his friends, nor spoke to them about 'our' Father. The exception was the Lord's Prayer, but even then it was made clear that the prayer was for *them* to pray, not for himself.

Evidently, Jesus was God's Son in a way that the disciples were not. It is in the Gospel of John that the eternal relationship between the Father and the Son is most clearly seen.

Postscript *Because of the weakness of men, we must distinguish between the standards set by our own fathers and God's perfect fatherhood. The fatherhood we have known, at its best, can only faintly mirror God's care and concern.*

By Adoption   Romans 8:14-17   Galatians 4:4-6
From Eternity   Luke 11:1-3   John 20:17   John 17:5,24

THOUGHT STARTERS

1 Study Galatians 4:1-7, which shows the contrast between slaves and sons (see verse 7). Trace, from verse 4, the processes by which the Christian has been made a child of God. What are the privileges that the Father gives to children?

2 How should our view of God as our Father affect the way that we pray? After thinking, check your reply with Matthew 7:9-11.

3 How would you answer a person who wasn't a Christian who claimed that God was the Father of all, and that there was no need to worry about prayer, the Bible, or church?

4 What do you think pleases God the Father most of all? What grieves him most? Compare your findings with Luke 15:11-24.

Winter, Upper New York State, U.S.A. 'Look at the birds . . . your heavenly Father feeds them' (Matthew 6:26).

GOD'S REVELATION

The Key Truth *'Revelation' means that God has spoken to us so that we can understand him and respond to his love.*

GOD REVEALS HIMSELF

Supremely in Jesus

Throughout history God has been communicating to mankind. In the Old Testament God sent messengers and prophets to speak his messages, but it is in Jesus Christ that his revelation is complete and perfect. This is why Jesus is called 'the Word'. He is the fullest way in which God has revealed himself to us. Jesus' life, his teaching and his character portrayed God perfectly, for he was God living as a man.

Through the Bible

Through a unique collection of writings, brought together over a period of about 1,500 years, God has made plain his plan for mankind, using men he guided to convey his message.

Some men were chosen to write selected history, others to communicate wisdom and worship, yet others to unfold the future, or to give instruction for belief and conduct. Every book has its individual way of showing us God, within the unity of the Bible.

Through creation

The universe communicates (in a more general way) its own message of the power and majesty of God to the human race.

Even those who have never read the Bible see the finger of God in the universe.

BIBLE CHECK

Jesus Hebrews 1:1-4 John 1:1-18; 14:8-10
Bible 2 Peter 1:19-21 Romans 16:25-27

In history

God has revealed himself in a powerful way through history. God's plan is revealed in the rise and fall of great empires, Egyptian, Babylonian or Roman. Jewish history is seen in the Bible as the means by which the Messiah would finally come.

Furthermore, it cannot be a coincidence that the beginning of the Christian faith took place at a historically stable time, when communications were excellent in the Roman Empire, and when there was one common language – Greek.

In man

God also reveals himself in the very way in which we are made up. Man is made in God's image, and this image, although distorted through deliberate rebellion, is not obliterated. As a result, man's nature can point to the work of the creator.

Man's complexity and creativity is a signpost of God's revelation, as also is the power of his conscience, his instincts and his emotions. It is evident that man was made to enjoy relationships, and these very relationships show the character of the God who made us.

Through human experience

God continues to speak to us in the present. His voice is heard in many ways: through human friendship, through the arts and through our appreciation of all that is beautiful.

Christ's followers are also given the Holy Spirit, who speaks both to individuals and churches, and who progressively transform those who listen to him. In these ways, God continues to reveal himself to men in the present.

Postscript *The creation tells us very generally about God. We can only know more about him, and know him personally, as we hear him speaking through Christ and the Bible.*

Creation Psalm 19:1-4 Romans 1:18-20
History Psalm 75:6,7 Daniel 2:44
Man Genesis 1:26,27 Psalm 139:13-16 Romans 2:14,15
Experience 2 Corinthians 3:17,18 Revelation 2:29

THOUGHT STARTERS

1 Consider carefully 2 Peter 1:16-21. What were the two ways in which Peter witnessed the truth of Christ? What encouraging features can you find in this passage about God's revelation? Compare verse 19 with Psalm 119:105.

2 According to Romans 16:25-27, what is the purpose of God's revelation?

3 Why does not everybody accept God's revelation in the various forms in which it comes? What does his revelation mean to you? See 2 Corinthians 4:3-6.

4 How do you explain kindness and bravery in people who have no belief in God at all?

'Anyone who will not receive the kingdom of God like a little child will never enter it' (Mark 10:15).

THE TRINITY

The Key Truth   *There is only one God. But God consists of three persons, the Father, the Son and the Spirit, who are all equally God.*

Assumed in the Old Testament

The Old Testament stresses that God is one. The prophet Isaiah, in particular, says that there is only one God, and that all other 'gods' are false. And yet, at the same time, the opening sentence of the Bible uses a plural form for God's name (*Elohim*), and does so hundreds of times subsequently.

There are enough indications in the Old Testament for us to recognise the idea of three persons within the Godhead. For example, God sometimes refers to himself as 'us', and there are appearances and visions of him which suggest different members of the Trinity.

Asserted in the New Testament

In the New Testament Jesus gives us some very clear teaching about the Father and the Spirit. We are left with these facts: there is one God – but the Father, the Son and the Spirit are all individually God.

The New Testament does not give us a formula about the Trinity, but the evidence is unavoidable. In the unity of the one God, there is a Trinity of persons achieving man's salvation, and in whose name we baptise.

Accepted by faith

Proof texts are not enough for a clear understanding of the Trinity. We must study all the teaching of Jesus and of his apostles, and observe the threads of truth that run through the Bible which relate to the *will* of the Father, the *work* of the Son and the inner working and *witness* of the Holy Spirit.

BIBLE CHECK

Assumed Isaiah 44:6-8 Genesis 1:26; 18:1-15
Asserted John 14:15-26; 16:5-15 Matthew 28:18-20

God the Father

The first person of the Trinity is called Father, not primarily because of his relationship to his creatures, but because of his relationship to the eternal Son.

It is the Father who predominates in the Old Testament. But even though this is true, God is seen as One, as Saviour, and as Spirit – in preparation for the fuller revelation of the three persons in one Godhead.

God the Son

The second person of the Trinity is called the Son. He became a man, Jesus Christ, in order to rescue men from the domination of sin. As Son of God he was involved with the Father in the creation of all things, and shared in his eternal glory.

Within the Trinity, the Son is subordinate to the Father, but only because of the work he does. Therefore the Son was sent by the Father, and only acted under his Father's authority.

God the Holy Spirit

The third person of the Trinity was sent from the Father in Christ's name, to make *personal* in the lives of Christians all that Christ had made *available* through the cross. Just as Jesus once lived among us, so the Spirit now lives in us.

Although he was active in the Old Testament, the Spirit's main task began after the ascension of Jesus. He is the one who points attention to Christ, who speaks to the church in every age, and who equips Christians with abilities to serve God.

Postscript · *The Trinity need not be a truth that has no relevance to our lives. We will understand the truth of the Trinity best as we experience the work of the Father, Son and Holy Spirit in our lives.*

Accepted   John 16:12,13   2 Corinthians 13:14   1 Peter 1:2
Father   Matthew 11:27   Luke 10:21   Acts 2:32-36
Son   John 1:1-18   Colossians 1:15-20   Hebrews 1:8
Holy Spirit   Romans 8:9-11   1 Corinthians 2:10,11

THOUGHT STARTERS

1 Read John 14:8-21. Go through this passage carefully and try to see how the different persons of the Trinity relate to one another, both in who they are and what they do.

2 Why did God not reveal the truth of the Trinity as clearly in the Old Testament as he did in the New? What does this tell us about the way God reveals himself?

3 Read Exodus 3:1-6. What can we learn from Moses' response to God as we think about the Trinity?

4 The teaching of the Trinity is much more than mere discussion over certain words. How can people make sure of benefiting practically from the teaching?

Iris Evansia, a three-petalled flower. 'May the grace of the Lord Jesus Christ, and the love of God, and the fellowship of the Holy Spirit be with you all' (2 Corinthians 13:13).

Jesus Christ

HIS INCARNATION

The Key Truth *The word 'incarnation' means 'to become human'. The New Testament tells us that God became a human being. This person, Jesus Christ, was fully God and fully man.*

Christ was Son of God before time and space

The Bible teaches that Jesus did not come into being when he was born, but that he has always existed as the Son of God. It was through him that God created the universe, and in him all things hold together.

It was by a supernatural conception

The circumstances of Jesus Christ's birth help us to understand that he was born without sin. The human bias to sin is inherited from our parents. Because of the unique conception of Jesus, he was born without this bias.

While Christ's birth was as normal as that of any human, his conception occurred through the intervention of the Holy Spirit. Because of this, Jesus was both God and man.

It upholds Christ's full deity

As the New Testament unfolds, the fact that Christ is God is increasingly revealed. The hints turn to signposts, and the signposts turn to bold acclamation.

The signposts are: Christ's *character* (his sinlessness and purity), his *claims* (to be the centre of all truth, to be the world's judge, and to have a unique relationship to the Father), and his *conduct* (in performing miracles, forgiving sins and accepting worship).

It establishes Christ's full humanity

The New Testament shows that Christ was fully

BIBLE CHECK

Before Time John 1:1-3 Colossians 1:15-17
Conception Matthew 1:18-25 1 Peter 2:22 Hebrews 4:15

human, born into a Hebrew family, and subject to the Hebrew law.

He experienced all the problems that people have to face. He was exposed to hunger and thirst, fatigue and sorrow, and he faced the full force of temptation – yet without ever giving way. Although he was still fully God, Jesus (as a man) shared completely the weaknesses of all men. Because of this, he was perfectly qualified to be the unique go-between, bringing man and God together.

It explains Christ's unique personality

Jesus Christ is without parallel, for he is both God and man, in two distinct natures, and one person for ever. It was the same Jesus who declared that he was thirsty, who also referred, in a prayer, to the glory which he shared eternally with the Father.

The New Testament writers do not try to explain, as a philosophy, how one personality could be both human and divine. But the portrait they give us identifies him both with man and with God.

It validates Christ's saving ministry

There are aspects of the incarnation that are beyond our understanding. But one thing is clear. We know enough to realise that in Jesus Christ, truly God and truly man, is found the one saviour that the human race needs.

By laying aside his eternal splendour, and involving himself in mankind's burdens – even to the point of death on the cross for our sins – he becomes the reconciler between God and man, and by his resurrection he brings our humanity to heaven.

Postscript *Errors have arisen in Christian history when either Christ's deity or his humanity has been neglected. It must be understood that in every way he is fully God and fully man.*

Deity John 8:46 John 8:50-58 Luke 5:20,21 John 20:26-29
Humanity Galatians 4:4,5 Hebrews 2:14-18; 5:7
Personality Matthew 8:24,27 John 19:28, 17:5
Ministry 1 Timothy 2:5 Philippians 2:5-11

THOUGHT STARTERS

1 Consider Colossians 1:15-20. How does this passage portray Christ in his relationship to creation, to the church, to God and to the cross?

2 People have argued over almost every aspect of Christ's incarnation. His full deity and full humanity have come in for particular attack. Why do you think this is, and what are the reasons for the limit to our understanding of this teaching?

3 In what ways should we follow the example of Jesus' life as a man? See Hebrews 12:2-4 for one possibility.

4 What do we gain from the fact that Jesus is, like us, a man? And what do we gain from the fact that, unlike us, he is God?

Hawaiian plant on volcanic deposit. 'He grew up before him like a tender shoot, and like a root out of dry ground' (Isaiah 53:2).

MAIN EVENTS IN THE GOSPELS

The Key Truth *The four Gospels present the reader with selected significant events in Christ's life. The following are of particular importance:*

His humble birth

Jesus was born during the reign of the Roman emperor Caesar Augustus, into an extremely poor family. He was born in alien surroundings during a Roman census, and he was born into immediate danger – as King Herod searched to kill him.

These two elements, the humility and insecurity of Jesus' birth, were to set the pattern of his whole life.

His sinless baptism

The baptism of Jesus marks the beginning of his ministry. John the Baptist was calling his hearers to a baptism of repentance. Jesus, however, had no sin of which he could repent. But by his submission to John's baptism, he showed his *identification* with sinful humanity. The descent of the Spirit like a dove and the Father's words of acceptance, which accompanied the baptism, came as God's approval of the ministry that was to follow.

His prolonged temptation

Immediately following his baptism, Jesus went into the desert for a period of forty days, during which he fasted, and was tempted by the Devil.

The temptations that are recorded for us took the form of challenging Jesus to by-pass his mission. Jesus successfully resisted these and all the other temptations that occurred throughout his life.

His revealing transfiguration

Towards the end of his public ministry Jesus took three of his disciples to a mountain-top where he

---

BIBLE CHECK

Birth Luke 2:1-7 Matthew 2:1-18 Luke 9:57,58
Baptism Matthew 3:13-17
Temptation Matthew 4:1-11

became brilliantly irradiated before them.

Moses and Elijah appeared, and spoke with Jesus about his coming ordeal in Jerusalem. The disciples also heard a voice of divine approval, as at Christ's baptism. The event was clearly a preview, in miniature, of Christ's glory that lay ahead.

His obedient death

The tide of events turned against Jesus after his triumphant entry into Jerusalem. The Passover meal that he celebrated with his friends was swiftly followed by his betrayal, by a series of unjust trials, by death on a cross and by burial.

It was a dark hour, but it was the hour for which Jesus had come into the world. He made it clear that he had come, not only to teach and heal, but also to suffer and die for all men.

His victorious resurrection

Thirty-six hours after the burial, Jesus' tomb was found empty, except for the discarded graveclothes. It was sufficient for John who 'saw and believed'.

Then Jesus began to appear to his friends over a period of forty days. This was not an illusion, for he took food, could be touched, and was seen alive by hundreds of people. And yet he was uniquely and powerfully different – the victor over death.

His glorious ascension

The last time the disciples were to see Jesus was on the Mount of Olives. He commanded them to make disciples everywhere and he promised them the gift of the Spirit, who would give them the power to do this. He was then taken from them, visibly. He would not be seen again until his return.

Postscript   *It is rewarding to compare the accounts of Christ's life in the four Gospels and to see how the writers, from their differing viewpoints, complement one another.*

Transfiguration   Luke 9:28-36
Death   Matthew 26 and 27   Luke 22:53
Resurrection   John 20 and 21   Luke 24:36-43
Ascension   Matthew 28:16-20   Luke 24:44-53

THOUGHT STARTERS

1 Read John 17:1-5. What exactly was the 'work' that Christ was given to do? How did the main events in his life contribute towards it?

2 From what we know, how did Jesus prepare himself for his main work? How did he prepare his disciples?

3 Jesus Christ had no home of his own, never travelled outside Palestine and never wrote a book. To what, then, do you attribute the impact that he has made upon the world?

4 'If only Christ were on earth today.' How do you react to this wish when it is expressed? Look at John 16:5-7.

Grindelwald, Switzerland. 'The Word became a human being, and, full of grace and truth, lived among us' (John 1:14).

MAIN ASPECTS OF HIS MINISTRY

The Key Truth *Christ was unlike any prophet or religious teacher that ever lived. By his authority and deeds and by the power of his teaching and his example, he challenged his hearers to believe in him as the unique Son of God.*

Authority that convinced

The authority with which Jesus taught amazed the people who heard him. The prophets of old repeatedly declared 'The Lord says . . .' But Christ's frequent phrase was 'But *I* say to you . . .' He directed his hearers towards himself.

The Jewish leaders of Jesus' day took their authority from the great teachers of the past, but Christ taught in his own name and authority.

Parables that provoked

The teaching of Jesus Christ was given in terms and images understood in daily life, and this is particularly true of his unforgettable parables which both concealed and revealed truth.

People would often be captivated by the story of the Runaway Son or the Rich Fool, only to discover that the parable had been about themselves.

Miracles that confirmed

Christ's authority was further demonstrated by his miracles. The wind and the waves were obedient to his command, and even the dead were brought back to life.

But most of his miracles were acts of healing that were part of his mission of love. They also pointed to his identity as the Son of God and to the coming of God's kingdom.

BIBLE CHECK

Authority Matthew 5:21,22,27,28,31-34; 7:24-29
Parables Mark 4:2 Matthew 13:10-17 Luke 15:11-32

Compassion that attracted

Christ's deep concern for people was born from his understanding that man is created in God's own image, but that man is also fallen and lives in a fallen world.

Because of this, Christ showed care and concern for the individual. This can be seen in his many encounters with the bereaved, the sick and the demon-possessed. The crowds were quick to recognise the high value that Jesus placed on the individual, and they came to him in large numbers.

Training that prepared

Towards the beginning of the second year of Jesus' public ministry, the twelve disciples were chosen to share in his work of teaching, preaching and healing. These men learnt from Christ's example and from the private instruction he gave them. He also trained them for their future work as they (and some seventy others) were sent out two by two to do his work.

The Twelve did not understand all that was being taught them at the time, but their training was to be vitally important in the future development of the church.

Controversy that challenged

From the outset the words and actions of Jesus had a controversial cutting edge that finally provoked a collision between himself and the Jewish authorities.

Jesus clashed with the Jewish leaders over the following issues: that he mixed with sinners, challenged traditions, liberated the sabbath, and that he claimed to be God.

Postscript *It is a remarkable fact that while Jesus directed his hearers towards himself, he never at any time gave the impression of being conceited, arrogant or selfish.*

Miracles Mark 1:23-28 John 10:31-33
Compassion Matthew 9:35-38; 15:32-39 John 11:30-44
Training Matthew 10:1-15; 16:13-21 1 John 1:1-4
Controversy Mark 2:5-7,15,16 Matthew 23:13-36; 26:62-66

THOUGHT STARTERS

1 Consider Jesus' teaching in Matthew 5:1-12. In what way did his words overturn the world's values? Try to list the blessings that belong to the members of Christ's kingdom.

2 How can a Christian best put into practice the attitude of Jesus to individuals? How can this be done in your own area?

3 The true Christian cannot avoid controversy. What issues need to be faced at present in the name of Christ?

4 What parable of Jesus has most spoken to you recently? Discuss this with some of your friends.

Anchor, Menai Strait, North Wales. 'We have this hope as an anchor for the soul, firm and secure' (Hebrews 6:19).

HIS NAMES

The Key Truth *The many different names of Jesus Christ reveal the distinctive characteristics of his person and the work that he came to do.*

Son of God

As no one else, Jesus taught his disciples to think of God as their Father in a particularly intimate way. But because of his use of the terms 'my Father' and 'your Father' it is clear that he saw his own relationship to the Father in a quite different way from that of his followers.

The Jewish authorities recognised this and accused Jesus of making himself equal with God. The term 'Son of God' occurs most frequently in John's Gospel.

The Word

The Old Testament tells us that God created all things by his word. He spoke and it came to be. The apostle John shows that this word was in fact God's Son, without whom nothing would exist.

The Word is also involved in God's creation in another important way. He is the perfect expression of God to men. Because Christ is the Word, he did not merely bring us God's good news, but he is himself that good news.

High Priest

This title, given to Christ in the book of Hebrews, is drawn from the Old Testament system of sacrifices. A sacrifice had to be made every year by the High Priest on behalf of God's people to atone for their sins.

Christ, by his sacrificial death (never to be repeated) is the perfect mediator and High Priest.

BIBLE CHECK

Son of God John 20:17; 5:18,25; 20:31
The Word Psalm 33:6-9 John 1:1-4, 14 Revelation 19:11-13

Messiah

For centuries the Jews had looked for a future King who would be a descendant of David. This person was called the 'Messiah' by the Jews (which in the Greek language is 'Christos', from which we get 'Christ'). He would have God's authority and power to bring in the end of the age and establish the kingdom of God.

It was Simon Peter who made the first clear declaration that Jesus was the Christ, but it is important to note that Jesus totally rejected the popular idea of the Messiah as being a political deliverer from the Roman Empire. He saw his messianic role as one of suffering and death for the salvation of men.

Son of Man

Jesus used this name more than any other to describe himself. Although it seems to speak of his humanity, in reality it is a pointer to his deity, for the term is drawn from the book of Daniel, where the Son of Man rules an everlasting kingdom.

Jesus used the title in three ways – when speaking of his *earthly ministry*, his *death* and his *coming glory*. It is suggested that he favoured this title because it carried no nationalistic associations, it implied an identification with *man*, and it had both 'overtones of divinity and undertones of humanity'.

Lord

To call Jesus *Lord* was, in the New Testament church, the mark of a true Christian. To use this name invited opposition – from the Jewish authorities on the grounds of blasphemy, and from the Romans on the grounds of treason against the Emperor. This was the name that ascribed *all* authority to Jesus.

Postscript *The very fullness of Christ defies human imagery and thought. The six titles described here are not the only ones the Bible gives to him. It is encouraging to list the numerous other titles given to Jesus.*

High Priest Leviticus 9:7,8 Hebrews 7:23-28
Messiah John 6:15 Matthew 16:16,21 John 4:25,26
Son of Man Daniel 7:9-14 Matthew 8:19,20; 20:17-19; 24:30
Lord 1 Corinthians 12:1-3 John 13:13 Philippians 2:9-11

THOUGHT STARTERS

1 Read Matthew 16:13-28. Jesus praises Peter for recognising him as Messiah, but then forbids that the identification be made public. Why? In what other ways is Jesus described in this passage, and how does he see his role?

2 In what ways is Christ superior to the Old Testament priesthood? Look at Hebrews 7:23-28.

3 Why do we bother about a title for Jesus Christ? What is the danger today in simply referring to him as 'Jesus'? Compare your answer with Mark 13:5,6.

4 Which, of Jesus Christ's many titles, has meant a lot to you? What new aspect of his person has come to light through this study?

Old lighthouse, Anglesey, North Wales. 'Jesus said, "I am the light of the world"' (John 8:12).

HIS ATONING DEATH

The Key Truth *The word 'atone' was coined by bringing the two words 'at one' together. This expresses its meaning. By dying for the sins of the world, Jesus Christ has made it possible for all men to be made 'at one' with God.*

CHRIST'S DEATH

Initiated a new relationship

The Bible teaches that man's sin has created a barrier of guilt between him and his creator. However, Jesus accepted the responsibility for human sin and willingly took its penalty on the cross. A new relationship is now available for those who respond to the good news that their sins can be forgiven.

Hostility has been replaced by friendship. Those who unite themselves to Christ are viewed by God as though they had never been rebels at all. Indeed, the Christian is seen as a new person altogether.

Fulfilled Old Testament scripture

The Old Testament showed that God and man could not be reconciled unless a sacrifice was made. Only then could the guilt of sin be removed.

The Old Testament animal sacrifices could not in themselves take away sin, nor could they be a final solution to the problem of sin. The New Testament sees them as illustrations of the perfect sacrifice Jesus was to make.

Destroyed Satan's kingdom

The power of Satan's kingdom was broken through the death and resurrection of Jesus Christ. The final destruction of the Devil is yet to be. The Christian is aware of his activity and influence – but is confident of victory and protection through the power of the cross.

BIBLE CHECK

New Relationship 2 Corinthians 5:15-19 Romans 5:8-11
Old Testament Hebrews 10:1-12 Isaiah 53:4-12

Reversed sin's dominion

In the Bible, the idea of redeeming (or 'buying back') a person who is enslaved is very strong. Christ is presented as the one who, by his death, redeems his people from the penalty of God's moral law.

Because Christ has taken our guilt upon himself, sin no longer has the power to dominate the life of the Christian.

Provided a way of victory

With the power of the Devil limited (and ultimately doomed), and with the guilt of sin removed, the cross of Jesus Christ has set the Christian free.

The Christian is not set free *from* the fight for moral purity – rather he is set free *for* the fight. The 'tenses' of salvation are as follows: we have been saved from the *penalty* of sin by a crucified Saviour; we are being saved from the *power* of sin by a living Saviour; we shall be saved from the *presence* of sin by a coming Saviour. From the cross onwards, the message is one of victory.

Guaranteed an eternity with God

The cross is the guarantee that God has set his eternal love upon his people; there could be no stronger demonstration than the death of his Son.

Death is still an enemy, but it is an enemy that is defeated because of the death and resurrection of Christ. Like the Devil, death will face ultimate annihilation. The cross assures the Christian of a promised inheritance in God's eternal kingdom.

Postscript *A great proportion of the four Gospels is taken up with the events surrounding Christ's death. The cross was not a tragic accident — it was the event to which Christ's whole life was directed.*

Satan's Kingdom Colossians 2:15 1 John 3:8
Sin's Dominion Galatians 3:13 Romans 6:6-11
Victory 1 John 1:7-9 Titus 2:14
Eternity Romans 8:31-39 Hebrews 2:14,15

THOUGHT STARTERS

1 Read Matthew 27:32-54. Consider Christ's death in terms of its fulfilment of the Old Testament (for example Psalm 22).

2 Just before he died, Jesus cried out 'It is finished!' (or 'accomplished' – John 19:30). What was the significance of this final saying? After thinking about this, read John 12:27 and 17:4.

3 What is the best response that a Christian can make to the sacrificial death of Jesus Christ?

4 In 1 Corinthians 1:18-25 we learn that the message of the cross is an offence to many. Why should this be so?

Rough stone cross, Norway. 'God demonstrates his own love for us in this: While we were still sinners, Christ died for us' (Romans 5:8).

HIS TRIUMPHANT RESURRECTION

The Key Truth   *The Bible says that God raised Christ from the dead. By doing this God declared that his Son was the Saviour of the world. The historical event of the resurrection is also the foundation of Christianity.*

The foundation of the Christian faith

The resurrection of Jesus Christ lifts Christianity from the level of philosophy, or a mere code of conduct, to the supreme stature of God's good news for the human race.

In the resurrection God set his seal of approval upon Christ as Son of God, and underlined the value of his death. It was the resurrection that transformed the followers of Jesus, and sent them out into the world to preach the good news. The resurrection is the pivot of the Christian faith.

An event supported by evidence

If we enquire into the evidence for the resurrection, we are confronted first by the *factual evidence.* There is the empty tomb, containing only the abandoned grave-clothes, and the persistent failure of all explanations other than that Christ had risen. Also to be faced are the numerous reported appearances of the risen Jesus, at different times and before different people.

There is also *the psychological evidence.* For example, there are the transformed disciples, the conviction of the early church in the face of persecution, and the change from Saturday to Sunday as the Christian day of worship (after centuries of Sabbath worship).

A promise of ultimate victory

If Christ had not been raised from the tomb, his death would have been evidence enough of the failure of his mission.

BIBLE CHECK

Foundation   1 Corinthians 15:12-19   Romans 1:4
Evidence   John 20:1-29   1 Corinthians 15:1-8

Thus the resurrection gives positive assurance that the Christian believer has not believed in vain. The mission of Jesus did not end in failure, but in triumph. Ultimately all things, even the 'last enemy', death itself, must submit to the victory and rule of Jesus.

The power of Christian experience

To the Christian, the resurrection of Christ is far more than a past event of history. It plays a vital part in Christian living in the present, and colours the outlook, hopes and motives of every believer.

The New Testament teaches us that Christians must be ready to be like Jesus Christ in his life and death. This means that when we are willing to die to self-interest (as Jesus died) then we will be able to live a new life (as Jesus rose to new life). The Christian lives and works in the very power by which God raised Jesus from the dead.

The assurance of eternal security

Christ's victory over death has made immense changes in the area of sorrow and bereavement. The finality has been taken out of death. All those who die can know that Christ has been through this experience before them, and will bring them through it to be with him.

Furthermore, because Christ's body was raised from death, the Christian has the guarantee that he too will receive in eternity a resurrection body of beauty and strength. This new body will be related to the old, but without weakness or decay.

Postscript *It is worth remembering that Jesus would never have risen from the dead so triumphantly if he had not first been willing to give up his life. We only receive God's new life when we give up the control of our own lives.*

Ultimate Victory   1 Corinthians 15:24-28   Acts 17:30,31
Christian Experience   Philippians 3:10,11   Romans 6:5-14
Eternal Security   John 11:25,26   1 Corinthians 15:20,42-57

THOUGHT STARTERS

1 Consider
1 Corinthians 15:1-11.
What are the main
points of emphasis in
the gospel proclaimed
by Paul? Try to list the
evidences for the
resurrection put
forward by Paul,
including the change
in himself.

2 How has the
message of Christ's
resurrection affected
your own view of
death and the future?

3 On the evidence
available, what kind of
body did Jesus possess
when he appeared to
his disciples after his
resurrection? Read
Luke 24:39-43.

4 Look at Galatians
2:20. What does this
mean, in practical
terms?

*Growing wheat. 'Unless
an ear of wheat falls to
the ground and dies, it
remains only a single
seed. But if it dies, it
produces many seeds'
(John 12:24).*

The Holy Spirit

HIS PERSON

The Key Truth *The Holy Spirit is the third person of the Trinity. He comes from the Father and the Son, and is equal with them. He is the one who actively carries out God's will and who works in the lives of Christians.*

He is the third person of the Trinity

The Holy Spirit is presented in the Bible as a person fully worthy of worship. Not only is he included in the Christian formula of baptism and in the apostolic blessing, but his works are described as the works of God.

He was associated with the work of creation; he gives the Christian new life; he is the source of all knowledge, the guide and helper of the church in all ages; and he makes salvation a real experience to individuals. Also, the apostle Peter equated lying to the Holy Spirit with lying to God (Acts 5:3,4).

When Christ had left the world, the Spirit was given his most specific work. The book of Acts (which is the account of the early church) portrays the Spirit as directing and controlling the new Christian movement.

He knows as a person (mind)

The Holy Spirit is more than a force; he is a person, with a character of his own. The Bible teaches that it is through the Holy Spirit that God knows us completely. It is the mind of the Spirit that helps to shape the life of the Christian.

Jesus declared that the Holy Spirit would *remind* the apostles of his words and teaching. The Spirit *speaks* (as in the letters to the seven churches of Revelation), *intercedes* and *assures* Christians that they belong to Christ.

BIBLE CHECK

Trinity Matthew 28:19   2 Corinthians 13:14   John 15:26
He Knows 1 Corinthians 2:10-12   John 14:26   Revelation 3:6

He feels as a person (emotion)

Because the Holy Spirit is a person, it is no surprise to discover that he can feel emotion, as we understand the term, for man has been made in God's image.

As a result, it is possible to make the Holy Spirit *sad*. He can also be *insulted* – and therefore we must be careful, in what we say and do, not to insult the Spirit who lives in us. The Bible challenges us to bring glory to God by the quality of our lives and characters. In this way we will please the Holy Spirit.

He acts as a person (will)

The same Spirit who was involved in the creation, who equipped God's leaders in the past and inspired the prophets, is the Spirit who came in power upon the early church, and acted in it and through it. Throughout the Bible we can see his active personality.

For example, the New Testament shows us that he convicts people of their sins (as happened on the day of Pentecost). He leads and instructs Christ's followers. At other points in the New Testament he forbids certain courses of action and appoints leaders for the church. In such ways we see that the Spirit is a person who acts decisively in executing God's plans.

Postscript *The ascension of Jesus and the coming of the Spirit at Pentecost meant that although Jesus was no longer visibly and physically present, the Spirit would be invisibly present with God's people everywhere. Christ now comes to every believer through the Holy Spirit. In having the Holy Spirit, we have Christ.*

He Feels Ephesians 4:30 Hebrews 10:29
He Acts John 16:8,13 Acts 8:29; 16:6; 20:28

THOUGHT STARTERS

1 Turn to John 16:5-15. It might have been imagined that Jesus' departure would be a disadvantage for his people. Why is this not true? From this passage, try to list the advantages of Christ's physical absence.

2 When were you aware, for the first time, that God the Holy Spirit was acting in your life? Compare your experience with others.

3 Why do we find that so many Christian people focus on Christ rather than on the Spirit? How do you react to this? See John 16:14.

4 How far is it possible for a Christian to know when the Holy Spirit has been pleased or displeased by certain actions or deeds?

Herring Gull. 'God gives us a spirit of power, of love and of self-discipline' (2 Timothy 1:7).

HIS NAMES AND DESCRIPTIONS

The Key Truth *The character and activities of the Holy Spirit are emphasised through the various names and descriptions by which he is known.*

HIS NAMES

The Holy Spirit

The third person of the Trinity is best known by this name. It was the name used by Jesus in his final words of promise to his disciples, and by Peter in his sermon on the day of Pentecost. The name conveys the Spirit's holiness and opposition to sin.

The Spirit of God

This title is used many times in both Old and New Testaments. It signifies both that the Spirit *is* God, and the he has God's power. Jesus claimed that it was by the Spirit of God that he confronted the demonic world of his day.

The Spirit of Christ

This title brings great comfort and assurance to Christian believers, because it shows us that Christ was true to his word by not leaving his followers desolate when he ascended to heaven. The Spirit was sent in fulfilment of Christ's promise: 'I will come to you'.

The Spirit of Truth

The apostles were assured that the Holy Spirit would enable them to remember Christ's teaching and lead them into all the truth. The reader of the Bible may be thankful for its trustworthy, divine authorship.

The Counsellor or Helper

The literal meaning of the term 'Counsellor' is *one who comes alongside*. This name is reassuring for Christians facing temptation, doubt, demanding service or opposition.

BIBLE CHECK

His Names Acts 2:32,33 Matthew 12:28 Romans 8:9 John 16:13,14 John 16:5-7

HIS DESCRIPTIONS

Wind

This vivid description of the Spirit's activity is used often in the Bible. There is Ezekiel's vision of the dry bones being given new life; there are Christ's words to Nicodemus in John 3, and the sound of rushing wind at Pentecost. The key ideas conveyed are mystery, sovereignty and energy.

Water

The chief reference to the Spirit's work as water comes from some words Christ spoke. Jesus talked about streams of life-giving water flowing from those who believe in him. He was clearly talking about the life-giving activity of the Holy Spirit.

Fire

The prophet Malachi predicts the coming of God's messenger in terms of refining fire, and this picture is picked up in the New Testament. John the Baptist said that Jesus would baptise with the Holy Spirit and with fire. It is possible that the tongues of flame at Pentecost were meant to show the Spirit's refining activity.

Oil

In the Old Testament, anointing with oil was a sign that God had chosen someone for a particular task. In this way, priests or kings were set apart for God's service. The Bible tells us that Jesus was 'anointed' by the Spirit, and this is also true of his followers.

Dove

The Spirit, in the form of a dove, descended upon Jesus at his baptism. While Jesus undoubtedly possessed the Spirit already, this event pictures the gentleness associated with the dove. This gentleness would characterise Christ's work.

Postscript *We must be careful not to press these images of the Spirit's work into being anything more than helpful pictures.*

His Descriptions   Ezekiel 37:1-14   John 3:8   John 7:37-39   Malachi 3:1-3   Matthew 3:10-12   Exodus 30:30   Acts 10:37,38   2 Corinthians 1:21,22   Mark 1:9-11   John 1:32,33

THOUGHT STARTERS

1 Read Acts 2:1-13. What impressions do you gain from this account? What three signs indicated that the era of the Holy Spirit had begun for the church? In what ways was Pentecost unique? What makes it the secret of the church's life?

2 Which of the names of the Holy Spirit do you warm to most in your experience? Why?

3 Single out one or more of the Holy Spirit's qualities, suggested by his description, and turn your discovery into prayer or thanksgiving.

4 At Pentecost, the apostle Peter links the gift of the Spirit to the gift of forgiveness (Acts 2:38,39). What may we learn from this about Christian communication?

Lleyn Peninsular, North Wales. 'The Spirit of God was hovering over the waters' (Genesis 1:2).

HIS WORK

The Key Truth   *The Holy Spirit is mainly featured in the Bible for his work in the lives of men and women. He is responsible for the following activities:*

He convinces of sin

Because the Holy Spirit knows as a person, it follows that the lives of individuals are open to his scrutiny. Our needs can be fully met by him, for he is God.

As Spirit of truth, his work is to convince the unbeliever of being wrong. This is not achieved by human means – it only takes place as the Holy Spirit makes the message of the Bible a living force in a person's heart and conscience. In this way, the Holy Spirit opens the eyes of men and women to their true spiritual condition.

He illuminates truth

As it was the Holy Spirit who inspired the writing of God's word, so it is he who shows us what the Bible means. He makes the words of the Bible understandable and relevant to our lives.

Without the enlightening work of the Holy Spirit, the truth of God's message remains misty, and can even appear nonsensical or offensive.

He reveals Christ

The apostles were taught that when the Spirit came in power upon them, his task would be to focus the spotlight not on himself, but on Christ.

This is the pattern of Christian experience. From Pentecost, the disciples became aware, not so much of the Spirit who was now controlling their lives, but of Christ and his love. It was indeed the Spirit of Christ who now ruled them.

BIBLE CHECK

Convinces John 16:8-11 Ephesians 6:17 Hebrews 4:12
Illuminates John 14:25,26; 16:13 1 Corinthians 2:12-14

He lives in believers

The Old Testament recognises that the Spirit works in a selective way, limiting his activity to certain individuals and tasks. But the prophets predicted a coming time when God would put his Spirit *permanently* within the lives of *all* his people. This prediction was finally fulfilled on the day of Pentecost.

The apostle Paul writes of *Christ* making his home in the hearts of his disciples, for it is the Spirit's work to make Christ real to the Christian. No one who belongs to Christ is without the Spirit. He empowers and equips us for the whole of life.

He inspires prayer

Because the Spirit is the Counsellor or Helper, we may look to him for assistance in all forms of Christian service and spiritual warfare.

In particular, the Spirit helps us to pray, because he understands our weaknesses. He prevents prayer from degenerating into mere mechanical drudgery or powerless routine.

He prepares for heaven

The entire Christian life is a life that is directed by the Spirit. The Christian has been set free from the control of sin, and God no longer judges him for it. However, although sin no longer controls, the disciple of Christ faces a life-long battle to develop a holy character.

It is the Spirit who helps a Christian in this battle and prepares him for the glory of heaven.

Postscript   *It is vital that we do not underestimate what takes place when the Holy Spirit enters a person's life and personality. All Christian growth happens because of him.*

Reveals John 15:26; 16:14   Acts 7:55
Lives Ezekiel 36:26,27   Ephesians 3:16,17   Romans 8:9-11
Inspires Romans 8:26   Ephesians 6:18
Prepares Romans 8:1-4,16,17   2 Corinthians 3:18

THOUGHT STARTERS

1 Look at Romans 8:1-17, which gives teaching on life in the Spirit. List what is accomplished in the Christian by the Holy Spirit. What is our duty (verses 12-17)? And what are our privileges?

2 If Christian discipleship is governed the Spirit, what is there left for us to do? Is Christianity an active or passive affair? Check your answer with Philippians 2:12,13.

3 What attitude should we have towards those who do not appear to appreciate, or respond to God's love? What is likely to bring a change in their outlook?

4 How may our resources for living be described? Compare your answer with 2 Corinthians 4:16.

Williamsburgh, Virginia, U.S.A. 'I pray that he may strengthen you with power through his Spirit in your inner being' (Ephesians 3:16).

HIS ACTIVITY IN THE CHRISTIAN

The Key Truth *From the beginning of our Christian discipleship, the Holy Spirit lives within us. He gives us the power to follow Christ, confidence in believing, and unity with other Christians.*

Life – new birth by the Spirit

Without the power of God, an individual is considered to be 'dead', spiritually. He shows no signs of life as far as God is concerned. The Bible teaches that the gift of new life is available because of the death of Christ on the cross.

This new birth is brought about by the Holy Spirit in the life of a person who responds to the good news of Christ. According to the Bible, that person can be described as a new being and an inheritor of God's kingdom. The new birth is not earned by personal achievement – it is God's free gift.

Assurance – the witness of the Spirit

The Holy Spirit comes to assure the Christian of the reality of his new relationship with Christ. He confirms that Christ's death will always be sufficient to provide complete forgiveness for sins.

He also confirms that the new believer is a child of God, and that the Bible's promise of eternal life is to be believed. The changing life and desires of the new Christian are a part of this inner witness by the Holy Spirit.

Unity – fellowship in the Spirit

Every Christian has received the Holy Spirit, and is said to have been 'baptised in the Spirit'. 'Baptism' includes the ideas of *entrance* and *membership*. The Christian is brought into the life of the Spirit at conver-

---

BIBLE CHECK

Life John 3:3-8   2 Corinthians 5:17   Titus 3:4-7
Assurance Romans 8:15,16

sion and is united to all other Christians in the body of Christ's church.

Ownership – the seal of the Spirit

The presence of the Holy Spirit in a person's life is the invisible yet permanent stamp of God's ownership upon that life.

Two ideas are present here. First, we *belong* to God – and therefore cannot be separated from his love. Second, we are given the guarantee that God will keep us *securely*. Eventually, God will claim his own people finally and completely.

Power – the fullness of the Spirit

Christians are commanded to be filled with the Spirit, as a continuous and regular experience. This is not something that only happens once. We are filled with the Spirit so that our lives may be holy and our work for Christ effective. To be filled, we must obey God and submit to his rule; we must turn from evil daily and depend upon God's power; we must give ourselves in the service of other people.

Confidence – the pledge of the Spirit

The Bible teaches that the Holy Spirit is given to the Christian as a foretaste of all that God has prepared for his people in the future.

As we experience a small part of the fullness of life that God will one day give us, the Holy Spirit encourages us to press on. He makes us more confident about the future God has planned for us.

Postscript   *A great deal of our life in the Spirit consists in living out and developing what God has already given us.*

Unity   Mark 1:8   1 Corinthians 12:13   Ephesians 4:3-6
Ownership   Ephesians 1:13,14; 4:30   Romans 8:38,39
Power   Ephesians 5:18   Acts 4:31
Confidence   2 Corinthians 5:5   1 Corinthians 2:9,10

THOUGHT STARTERS

1 Read Paul's prayer in Ephesians 3:14-21. What is the 'power' that he desires for his friends? Where does this power come from, and what will it do for us?

2 Look at verse 20 of the same chapter. What instances can you recall in Christian history, or from your own experience, that illustrate these words of Paul?

3 Which of the different blessings of the Holy Spirit has meant the most to you?

4 Why is there no instance in the Bible of any individual claiming publicly to be filled with the Spirit – although this was sometimes stated *about* an individual by those who knew him? Read Acts 6:1-6.

Hakone, Japan. 'Whoever believes in me, streams of living water will flow from within him' (John 7:38).

HIS FRUIT

The Key Truth *It is the work of the Holy Spirit to transform our characters. The qualities listed below are developed in us by the Spirit and are taken from Galatians 5:22,23*

Love

Christ said that his 'new' commandment was that we should love one another. It was new because the love he had in mind was modelled on his own – a selfless, sacrificial and practical love that is revolutionary in any age.

Joy

The person who is reading the Bible for the first time will be surprised to find that joy and persecution go hand in hand in numerous instances (e.g. Matthew 5:11,12; Acts 5:41; James 1:2,3; 1 Peter 4:12-14).

This kind of New Testament joy is totally independent of circumstances. It is the joy of Christ's reign in our lives, inspired by the Spirit.

Peace

The peace which 'passes all understanding' was described by Jesus to his disciples as 'my' peace. It does not mean the absence of trouble, but the deep peace that protects the life that is hidden in Christ.

Patience

The apostle Paul longed for the readers of his letters to be tolerant and patient in the face of each other's faults. Peter pointed to the example of Christ's endurance and patience under suffering. The strongest kind of patience comes only from Christ.

Kindness

Wherever the Spirit of Christ is involved in a situation

BIBLE CHECK
Love 1 Corinthians 13 **Joy** 1 Peter 1:3-9
Peace John 14:27 **Patience** 1 Peter 2:23
Kindness Titus 3:1-5,8

or person, kindness will be seen in action. We can see Christ's unique brand of kindness in his parables, in his breaking of conventions to help the outcast, and in the value he placed on the individual.

Goodness

It was the transparent goodness of Jesus that drew people to him long before his true identity was known. Goodness is love in action. It expects no rewards, and it stems from a heart of purity and openness. It points other people to God.

Faithfulness

God delights to give his servants responsibilities. As we are faithful in the small tasks God gives us, he will trust us to do greater things. The Bible reminds the Christian servant of the final day when the faithfulness of his service will be assessed.

Gentleness

Once again, the Bible shows us that true gentleness was seen in Jesus Christ. In the face of extreme provocation he never lost control and never flaunted his immense power. His disciples needed to learn this quality – notably James and John (Luke 9:51-56).

Self-control

Excess and a lack of discipline result from moral weakness, while self-control is a sign of strength and growth in character. Paul said that we should be like athletes, who go into strict training before a sporting event. Thus, when the Spirit is in control, we experience the difference he makes.

Postscript   *We should recognise that natural gifts in the Christian are enhanced, rather than diminished, by the work of the Holy Spirit.*

Goodness   1 Peter 2:11,12
Faithfulness   Matthew 25:14-30
Gentleness   Matthew 11:28-30
Self-Control   1 Corinthians 9:24-27

THOUGHT STARTERS

1 Read and think about 1 Corinthians 13. Why is love of this kind so vital, and so revolutionary? How may it be developed in an individual – and in a fellowship?

2 Go through Galatians 5:22,23 and discover whether these qualities can be grouped under different categories. For example, fruit that relate to God, to others, etc.

3 Try to list some people in the Bible who had obviously developed one or more of the fruit of the Spirit.

4 Why do the Bible translations that mention 'fruit' in Galatians 5:22, not make the word plural – 'fruits'? How does the Christian develop these qualities – one by one, all together, instantaneously, painfully?

Apple blossom. 'No branch can bear fruit by itself; it must remain in the vine. Neither can you bear fruit unless you remain in me' (John 15:4).

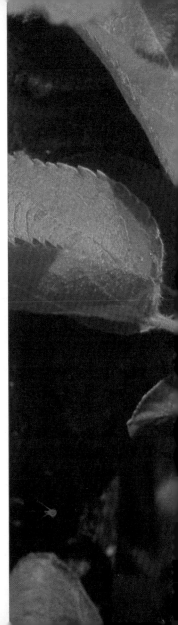

HIS GIFTS

The Key Truth *The Holy Spirit distributes among Christians a variety of spiritual gifts, which are to be used for the building up of Christ's body, the church. No believer is without a gift.*

The gifts exalt Christ

While the 'fruit' of the Spirit is concerned with charac-ter, the gifts of the Spirit relate to abilities and func-tions distributed among believers. All the fruit should be exhibited in every Christian but the gifts differ widely from person to person.

The hallmark of spiritual gifts is that they glorify Christ. The Holy Spirit was sent for this very purpose – to illuminate the Lordship of Jesus.

The gifts involve all

Four passages of scripture list some of the gifts: *Romans 12:6-8; 1 Corinthians 12:8-10; Ephesians 4:11,12; 1 Peter 4:10,11.*

It is significant that the gifts of the Spirit are not restricted to outstanding individuals, or leaders in the church. Each believer has at least one gift, and these gifts are to be discovered and developed, for all God's people are to be involved in Christian ministry and service of some kind.

The gifts should unite all

The church of Christ is likened to a body, composed of many limbs and parts, each part relating to the whole.

The individual believers, then, should see the abilities and functions that God has given them as gifts available for the whole body. In this respect, Paul had to correct the divided Corinthian church.

BIBLE CHECK

Exalt Christ   1 Peter 4:10,11   John 16:14
Involve All   1 Corinthians 12:7-11

Gifts lay foundations

The church of Christ is also likened to a building, built upon the unique and powerful ministry of the apostles and prophets, Christ himself being the stone that holds the whole building together.

The gifts which characterised the apostles may not be in evidence today in the highest sense of those callings, but there are Christians who in a secondary sense have been *sent* (as the apostles) to establish the church across new frontiers, or who *speak* to the church in relevant terms (as the prophets) to encourage and build it up.

Gifts build up the fellowship

There is a great variety of spiritual gifts featured in the New Testament. The Christian is to make careful use of every gift received, to build up harmony and unity in the fellowship.

It is import that individual believers are not jealous of the gifts of others, nor insist on the superiority of their own. As we use God's gifts, we should be humble and look for ways in which we can serve others.

Gifts promote mission

The gifts of the Spirit are given for more than building up the church – they are given to widen its boundaries.

However corrupt and challenging their environment, Christ's followers are called – individually and collectively – to use their gifts in proclaiming the good news, vigorously co-operating with the Spirit of God in making mature disciples.

Postscript *Everyone has 'natural' gifts from birth, which are given by God. By giving these back to him, they can be enhanced and made use of by Christ as they learn to follow him.*

Unite All   Romans 12:4,5   1 Corinthians 12:12-26
Lay Foundations   Ephesians 2:19-22
Build Up   Ephesians 4:11-13
Mission   Colossians 1:27-29   1 Corinthians 14:24,25

THOUGHT STARTERS

1 Look at Romans 12. What does Paul teach us about the way in which we use our gifts, and our attitude to other Christians? What difference should this passage make to your local church?

2 What is the best way of discovering what your gifts are, as a Christian? How can other Christians help you to do this?

3 How far is your own fellowship using the gifts of everyone to promote Christ's mission in the world? Identify any gifts that are being neglected in this respect, and that can be encouraged.

4 Why do certain abilities or gifts sometimes cause problems for a church, as they seem to have done at Corinth?

Pennant Valley, North Wales. 'Live by the Spirit' (Galatians 5:16).

Man

HIS UNIQUENESS

The Key Truth *The Bible tells us that man is the summit of God's creation. He is the only being who may enter into a personal relationship with the creator.*

MAN IS

A whole being, physical and spiritual

The Bible teaches that all men have a common origin and nature. Man was created as an intelligent being and is recognised as the head of all living things. As such, he is to govern the earth and to use its resources responsibly.

Because of man's place in creation, God made him as a physical being, completely involved in God's world. But man is not merely physical. He also has a spiritual dimension – he can be fully aware of God and all that he demands. These two dimensions, physical and spiritual, make up the whole person.

This description of man is given in the biblical account of creation, which, in its scope, simplicity and dignity, is without parallel anywhere in literature.

A spiritual being, made in God's image

What characterises man as unique is his creation in the image and likeness of God. He possesses a similar nature to God and is therefore capable of a relationship with his maker.

Because man is made in God's image, this does not mean that he *is* God, or even that he is a part of God. The Bible clearly teaches that man is distinctly different from God. Therefore man is not God in disguise, nor is he an 'incarnation' of God. But there is in man a key element that sets him apart from, and above nature. He has been made to love God, to worship him and to enjoy his company.

BIBLE CHECK

A whole being Acts 17:26 Genesis 2:15,19,20 Matthew 4:4
A spiritual being Genesis 1:26,27 Psalm 8:3-6

A personal being, with mind, emotion and will

Man is not only made for God. He is also made for a variety of personal and loving relationships within the human family. His spirit reveals qualities of tenderness, loyalty and self-sacrifice. He is capable of original thought and of intelligent choice. He is fully aware of himself, capable of humour, sorrow, or hatred. He appreciates beauty and enjoys recreation.

The qualities of man show that he is not an animal or a machine. His instincts, affections and aspirations prove that he is far removed from being a mere collection of chemical reactions. The Bible recognises that he has the dignity of personality and freedom.

A moral being, responsible for his actions

The Bible assumes and teaches that man has a moral aspect, which relates him to his creator. This may be seen in the laws which govern even the most primitive societies. Man recognises the difference between right and wrong.

The animal kingdom behaves according to the drive of instinct. Man possesses a drive that makes him morally aware – a drive which says *'I ought.'*

As a result, it is basic to the teaching of the Bible that man is not a victim of his upbringing or circumstances. Rather, he is responsible for his actions and must answer for them. If we remove this concept from our understanding of man's nature, we also remove any true content from such words as reward, merit, justice and even forgiveness.

Postscript *It is the dimension of God in man's being that raises him above the level of an animal, a machine or an accident.*

A personal being Genesis 2:18 Luke 10:25-37
A moral being Romans 2:14,15 Psalm 51:1-3

THOUGHT STARTERS

1 Read Psalm 8. What gives significance to man in the vastness of the surrounding universe? What do we learn of his position and status, and of his responsibilities? In what way does this Psalm correct current errors of thinking?

2 A famous film star once said, 'I am just a piece of meat.' From the Bible, how may we comment on and correct such a statement?

3 Look at Genesis 1:26,27. In what ways do you think man is like God? In what ways is man unlike him?

4 How do you react to the belief that wrong-doing is a kind of disease, for which there is, somewhere, a proper form of treatment? May this sometimes be true?

Steam traction engine, England. 'What is man . . . you crowned him with glory and honour and put everything under his feet' (Hebrews 2:6–8).

HIS DIVERSITY

The Key Truth *The many different sides of man show positively that man was created by God, and for God.*

Natural dimensions

God has given mankind the earth as a home to live in and to look after. It is a home that is teeming with life and overflowing with variety and colour. Its seasons are regulated and its resources are immense.

The world and matter are not evil (as various non-Christian teaching have maintained) but are part of God's good creation. Food and bodily health are the gifts of God and are to be received with thanks. Through farming and agriculture, man is to be productive in the home that God has given him.

Creative dimensions

In general it is true that when the scriptures have been taken seriously, technology and science have flourished in a productive way. This is because the Bible encourages man to explore and develop the wonderful works of God. Mining, trade and manufacture, performed responsibly, are a part of man's task during his stay on the planet.

Cultural dimensions

Man possesses what the animal kingdom can never know – a capacity for the appreciation of what is beautiful, for intellectual development, for literature and the arts and for sport and recreation.

Life on earth is meant to be enjoyable, but cultural activity calls for as much discipline as any other part of life. Nevertheless, rest and re-creation are a vital part of the programme of man.

Social dimensions

Man was placed on the earth to live not in isolation

BIBLE CHECK

Natural Genesis 8:22   Psalm 104:5-30   1 Timothy 4:3,4
Creative Genesis 1:26-28; 9:1-3   Psalm 8:6-8

from his neighbour, but in the pattern of community and family that stems from God's own nature. God has made us for relationships.

The Bible points out the enormous value of friendship, and above all, marriage. The relationship between a husband and wife is seen as a gift from God. Through shared problems and pleasures, companionship and the joy of sexual intimacy, married partners are able to strengthen each other throughout life.

We have been created to show compassion and justice in the way we treat others. Only when man uses these qualities do his relationships in the family, in social care, in government and in work become what God meant them to be. God's ideal for all people is that they should love one another.

Religious dimensions

Man was made by God, and he has a spiritual capacity. As he is far from God, he constantly searches for his spiritual home. The search takes many forms, which are seen in the great religions of the world, in the human quest for oneness with God, and for an experience which materialism is unable to give.

Jesus confirmed both an Old Testament saying and the findings of the human heart when he declared that 'Man does not live on bread alone' (Matthew 4:4). Man needs more than the physical essentials of life. It is the Bible that gives to searching humanity the answers that philosophers and learned men of religion have always been unable even to guess at: that God was on a search himself – for man whom he loves.

Postscript   *Man's immense powers should inspire us to develop to the full our potential for creative service in this world.*

Cultural Exodus 35:30-35   Daniel 1:3,4
Social Genesis 2:18-24   Romans 13:8-10
Religious Psalm 90:1   Ecclesiastes 3:11

THOUGHT STARTERS

1 Read 2 Corinthians 5:1-10. How does the apostle Paul view his physical existence; his heavenly future; and the experience of being linked to both?

2 What natural abilities has God given you? How have they enriched you as a person? What is the danger of having many natural abilities?

3 How do you see your role in a society that is often corrupt? As one of involvement, separation, compromise, condemnation? Check your answer with John 17:15,16 and Matthew 5.13-16.

4 At times in history, Christians have looked distrustfully at the arts. Why is this so? What principle should govern us in our attitude to music, painting, films and literature?

The old city, Stockholm. 'He himself gives all men life and breath and everything else' (Acts 17:25).

HIS REBELLION AND FALL

The Key Truth   *God in creation gave man the gifts and privileges that allowed him individuality and freedom. The wilful misuse of these led man into rebellion and his subsequent fall.*

Man's innocence gave him fellowship with God

'Innocence' is the correct word to use of man's original moral state. He was not *righteous,* in the sense of possessing a developed uprightness of character; rather he was child-like in the trusting and open simplicity of his walk with God.

Man's innocence was not an in-built and unalterable characteristic. He was not programmed to obey his maker, in the way that a computer must function – for man was not like a machine. He was a person, living in a free relationship with God.

Unlike his descendants, man originally had no inward urge to sin. But whether or not he was to remain in a relationship with God depended upon the choices that he could freely make.

Man's freedom gave him the power of choice

The Bible reveals that man was a free agent in regard to his relationship with God. He was not obliged to go God's way. In any true relationship the people concerned must have the freedom of choice that raises them above the level of being robots or puppets.

God did not hide from man that he had the power of choice. The instructions given to him were clear enough. He was free to choose.

Man's choice gave him true responsibility

Although we are influenced by other people in what we do, ultimately, *we* must take the responsibility for the decisions we make. To have the ability to choose

---

BIBLE CHECK

Fellowship   Genesis 2
Choice   Genesis 2:16,17; 3:6,7

between right and wrong means that we also have the responsibility to choose what is right.

In the story of man's fall, we see how people try to avoid this responsibility. Adam blames Eve, who in turn blames the serpent. By the way that God deals with each of them, he shows that they were all guilty for the sins that they had committed.

Man's decision led him into moral rebellion

Man's revolt against his creator cannot be described as an accidental slip. Man questioned God's authority by disobeying him, and he doubted whether God really knew what was best for him. As a result, he deliberately rebelled against God and followed his own way.

What man thus became – a sinful and fallen being – mankind is today. Estranged from the creator, the human race as a whole must be described biblically as a fallen race. It is not that the image of God in man has been completely destroyed. It is still there, although distorted and marred. But there is no area of man's mind and personality that does not exhibit a degree of 'fallenness'.

The sin principle has become universal. Men and women today, from their actions and choices, underline their involvement with the fallen race.

Postscript *The fallenness of man means that for the whole of our lives we have a tendency to rebel against God. All mankind is on the same level of need.*

Responsibility Genesis 3:8-19 Matthew 12:36,37
Rebellion Genesis 3 Psalm 51:5 Jeremiah 17:9

THOUGHT STARTERS

1 Read and study the Ten Commandments (Exodus 20:3-17). Why did we need the Law to be given at all? What areas of life do these commandments deal with? Why are they still relevant today? Do you know them by heart?

2 Whose fault is it, when we do wrong? The Devil's? God's – for having given man free choice? Our 'fallen' nature? Compare your findings with Genesis 3:11-13; Romans 1:20; 3:19,20.

3 How can Christ's followers strengthen their desire to choose the good and not the evil?

4 We are responsible for everything that we choose to do. Describe, in your own words, what responsibility means. What does this tell us about the God who made us?

Ruined quarry, North Wales. 'Their thoughts are evil thoughts; ruin and destruction mark their ways' (Isaiah 59:7).

HIS REBELLION AND CONDEMNATION

The Key Truth *It is disastrous that man has rebelled against the creator, for God in his absolute holiness will not tolerate sin, but must condemn the sinner. As a result, man is guilty, confused, and separated from God.*

Rebellion and guilt

God made man to live in relationship with all of humanity on a collective basis. Therefore, it is not surprising that scripture teaches that the whole race is involved in the original fall, although no man is condemned for the sin of any other person.

Because we have rejected goodness and follow our own way rather than God's, we are guilty before him. Guilt is both a feeling and a fact. It is a *feeling* because our consciences tell us when we have done wrong. We feel ashamed and guilty for what we have done.

It is a *fact* because God knows that we have rebelled against him. We are guilty in the same way that a criminal has been proven guilty. We deserve God's judgement.

Guilt and condemnation

The effects of man's revolt against the authority of God are inescapable. In Genesis chapter 3, man and woman are sent away from Eden and are told that they will only be able to live off the earth by hard work.

God had no choice but to condemn mankind. Because of his justice and holiness he cannot tolerate evil. Therefore, when God condemns us he shows that he is taking our sin seriously. To be condemned is to experience the anger of God.

Condemnation and separation

Although man comes under certain limitations as a result of his rebellion, the Bible emphasises that his

---

BIBLE CHECK

Rebellion and Guilt   Romans 5:12-17   Ephesians 2:1-3
Guilt and condemnation   Psalm 14:2,3; 143:2

main loss is spiritual. His most precious privilege – that of free access to God and fellowship with him – has been forfeited.

Throughout the history of man, and that of God's people, it is sin that has created barriers between sinful humanity and the holy God. Man finds himself confused by his own capacity for evil and out of place in this world because he is separated from God.

Estranged from God, man is ignorant of his maker and of his ways, and is unable to fulfil his destiny. He cannot enter into peace with God, and he cannot undo the past.

Separation and death

'The Tree of Life' in Genesis 2 conveys the idea of the eternal life of God. When man fell out of fellowship with God he was deprived of such life. The Bible teaches that sin and death are linked to each other.

The apostle Paul declares that death is the payment we receive for sinning. The difference between death as a spiritual state, and death as the end of physical existence is not always clearly drawn in scripture. Spiritually and physically, death is an outrage in the teaching of the Bible, because it is God's judgement upon sin. As such, it could never be abolished but by the action of God.

The physical conquest of death by Jesus Christ overshadows all else in our understanding of this issue.

Postscript *Because of the universality of sin, it is all too easy to become used to locks, keys and tickets, and other daily reminders that fallen man is not to be trusted.*

Condemnation and separation Genesis 3:23,24
Isaiah 59:1,2
Separation and death Genesis 2:15-17   Ezekiel 18:4
Romans 6:23

THOUGHT STARTERS

1 Read and examine Psalm 51, written by David after an incident in 2 Samuel 11 and 12. How does David understand God's attitude to sin; the nature of sin; the remedy (both short-term and long-term – see Ezekiel 36:25-27); and his owm right attitude for the future?

2 Why are terms such as sin, guilt and the fall of man not fashionable in some circles today? Were they ever fashionable?

3 Christians are people with joy in their hearts. How is it possible to live with the biblical concept of our fallenness and yet to avoid dwelling constantly on our own failures?

4 What are the practical indications from man and his surroundings that this world, while still a good place to live in, has lost its initial perfection?

The ruins of a Greek temple. 'All have sinned and fall short of the glory of God' (Romans 3:23).

HIS QUEST AND DILEMMA

The Key Truth *The history of the human race tells us about man's quest for the meaning of his existence. Men will remain in confusion, unless they experience the light and life of God. This confusion is seen in the following areas:*

His religious search

Man is continually torn between the revelation of God, culminating in the person of Christ, and the numerous human attempts (frequently including valuable insights and much that may be admired) to make a path to God.

These attempts have taken many forms in history, ranging from primitive superstition and magic to powerful and sophisticated religious systems.

In Bible times, God's leaders were continually challenging their hearers to forsake the man-made ways to God, and to accept the revelation of the one and only Lord. Many of the New Testament letters highlight the issue of false teachers and religious trails that lead to idolatry and error.

His philosophical wanderings

The way of philosophy is the age-old search for the elusive wisdom and knowledge about the ultimate reality of the universe. Most attempts arrive at different conclusions, and some arrive at none.

The conclusions of philosophy (when God's revelation had been left out of the picture) is perfectly mirrored in the Old Testament book of Ecclesiastes. The writer shows that man's mind, without the help of God, is unable to come up with convincing answers to the meaning of life.

His psychological contradictions

Man's nature constantly comes into collision with his state as a fallen being. Because he was created in the

---

BIBLE CHECK

Religion Acts 17:22,23   2 Timothy 4:3,4
Philosophy Ecclesiastes 1:16-18   1 Corinthians 1:20,21

image of God, man was designed to enjoy the company of his maker. His instincts will not easily allow him to forget his origin and his capacity for rational and satisfying relationships.

However, his fallenness and state of enmity with God make him a mass of contradictions. For man is not only at war with God. History all too frequently has shown him to be at war with his neighbour, with his environment, within his family and with himself.

Man's problems do not stem so much from his outward circumstances, as from his own inner state. Jesus taught this, and so did his apostles. True identity and significance continue to elude all those who do not know God. Hence the symptoms of disorder. Hence the need of a Redeemer.

His physical drive

Besides the loss of harmony in man's emotions, will and relationships, the Bible points to the abnormal predominance of his physical and sensual appetite as being a result of the fall.

Thus, history's periods of spiritual poverty have tended to coincide with a marked increase in society's dependence upon money, alcohol, promiscuity and dehumanised pleasure.

Man has great potential for creativity and technical advance, but when this is not controlled by a God-centred view of the world, indiscipline and slavery are the inevitable result.

Postscript *The Christian who fails to grow spiritually is liable to be caught up in the very dilemmas that ensnare the world, and lose his assurance of peace with God.*

Psychological Mark 7:21-23 James 4:1-4 Romans 7:18-24
Physical Ephesians 4:17-19 Titus 3:3

THOUGHT STARTERS

1 Look at James 4:1-10, for a picture of people who are in open rebellion against God. What characterises their actions, and what explains them? What is the road to spiritual recovery, and what *encouragements* are there in this passage?

2 What examples are there, in your own area, of people searching for religious answers to life? How can your church best contribute to their search? Compare your findings with 1 Thessalonians 1:5.

3 As a Christian, can you recall what it was still to be in ignorance of God's friendship? How far did Revelation 3:17 describe you?

4 List the ways in which man is at war with himself, his neighbour, nature and God.

Man silhouetted on rock. 'Can you fathom the mysteries of God? Can you probe the limits of the Almighty?' (Job 11:7).

HIS ENEMIES

The Key Truth   *As a result of his fall, man finds himself faced by real and powerful enemies that can only be overcome by the greater power of God.*

Satan

The Devil is not all-powerful or present everywhere at once, as God is. He is a created spirit or angel, who chose to rebel against the authority of God, and who fell from heaven.

He is the enemy of man (the word Satan means 'opponent' or 'enemy'). *His aim* is to humiliate man, to separate him from God, and to destroy him. *His power* is immense, but limited. He is a deceiver, a liar, a tempter and a murderer. He is described in scripture as a roaring lion and as a dragon.

His defeat was achieved through the death and resurrection of Jesus, and will be completed when he is finally judged and destroyed by Christ. *Meanwhile, the Devil is to be resisted* (James 4:7).

Sin

Sin came into the world through the Devil, and became universal in the life of man through the fall. Sin is defined in the Bible as breaking the law of God, as enmity with God, as rebellion, and as falling short of God's standard.

The outbreak of sin reveals itself in a great variety of ways, sometimes in gross acts, but equally powerfully in the subtle undermining of will, motivation and character. As a Christian focuses on Christ, so his determination to fight against sin is strengthened. *With Christ's help sin isto be rejected* (Hebrews 12:1,2).

The world

By the 'world' the Bible frequently means the society, system and outlook which is hostile to God and limits

---

BIBLE CHECK

Satan 1 John 3:8   1 Peter 5:8,9   Revelation 12:7-12
Sin 1 John 3:4   Romans 3:23; 8:10

life to earthly existence only. Those who live in this way limit their desires to gaining possessions and position, and exclude God altogether.

The results of living by this philosophy are all too evident in the life of mankind, and the Christian can be powerfully tempted by the things he sees in the world. However, he can take courage in the defeat of the world by Jesus. *Meanwhile we are to shine as a light in the world* (Philippians 2:15).

The flesh

Apart from its usual meaning, 'flesh', often termed 'sinful nature' or 'human nature' in modern Bible translations, refers to the sinful bias which every individual has. This sinfulness is found in both obvious and hidden selfish indulgence.

Man possesses this fallen human nature throughout life. As the Christian also possesses Christ's Spirit, but is still in the flesh as well, he becomes something of a battleground between flesh and spirit. *However, we learn to live according to the Spirit and not the flesh* (Romans 8:9).

Death

Death is man's great enemy, pursuing him from infancy, disturbing his peace and haunting his hopes. However, the Christian recognises that Christ is the great destroyer of death and of the very fear of death. Like others, the Christian faces life's problems and trials, *but he gives thanks to God who gives him victory through Jesus Christ* (1 Corinthians 15:57).

Postscript *A subtle temptation for the Christian is to blame personal failures on the Devil or on the pull of the world. When we sin, it is because we have chosen to do so.*

The World 1 John 2:15,16 James 4:4 John 16:33
The Flesh Romans 7:18 Galatians 5:17
Death 2 Timothy 1:10 Hebrews 2:14,15 Revelation 21:4

THOUGHT STARTERS

1 Read Ephesians 6:10-18, and think about the Christian's defences against spiritual opposition. List the commands in this passage – *Put on*, etc. How do you interpret the various pieces of armour? Why may we expect to win?

2 Whose world is it – the Devil's, or God's? Compare your findings with 1 John 5:19; Matthew 4:8,9; 1 Samuel 2:8; Psalm 24:1 and Revelation 11:15.

3 Specify different situations when the Christian should run from evil, meet it head-on, undermine it, or stand firm?

4 In what way is man always changing? In what way does he remain the same?

Street in Cologne. 'Do not conform any longer to the pattern of this world' (Romans 12:2).

Salvation

GOD'S PLAN FOR MANKIND

The Key Truth *God has always had a plan for rescuing those who are in rebellion against him. The Bible tells us that although we are free to respond to God, he has already chosen us to be his people. The word 'predestination' means that God has selected and separated a people for himself.*

God's plan – his will is sovereign

The Bible teaches that God is above everything, and he uses the most unlikely people to carry out his purposes.

Thus, Jacob and not Esau (who was the older of the two) was chosen to be head of the family which God would use to rescue man. Similarly David, the youngest of his family, was chosen as the one through whose descendants the Messiah would come. In the New Testament, those who were called to be God's people in Christ were called purely on the basis of God's own purpose and generosity.

God's plan – his work is eternal

The Bible teaches us that God's work of salvation, centring in Christ, has been planned from eternity.

The death of Jesus in Jerusalem at a fixed point in time was the result of the wilful act of angry men, but it must also be seen as an event planned by God from before the beginning of the world.

God's plan – his choice is specific

While the Bible is against the idea of 'fatalism' (that is, whatever God decides for us, we are fated to do), it does teach that God's plan is more than simply a general call to all mankind. Those who freely respond to his call learn that God had chosen them from among many, according to his own purpose and will.

BIBLE CHECK

Sovereign 1 Corinthians 1:26-29 Romans 9:10-18
Eternal Acts 2:23 1 Peter 1:18-20 Revelation 13:8

God's people – separated for holy living

Properly understood, the biblical teaching of predestination will never generate complacency in those who are chosen by God. For the people of God are called to be *holy*.

In the Old Testament, something that was specially set apart for the service of God was called 'holy'. So it is with the Christian. On freely responding to God's call, we learn that we have been predestined, from eternity, for a life of obedience and Christ-likeness.

God's people – called to good works

God's call of Abraham, of Isaac and Jacob, was for the specific purpose of bringing benefit to the world.

God's people, in the New Testament, are called to a life of good deeds and energetic mission. It is not for them to determine who are among the called. Their responsibility is to proclaim and reflect the goodness of God to all of humanity.

God's people – preparing for future glory

God's eternal plan for his people has a glorious future in view. From the beginning, the Christian has been chosen for salvation; this includes the future life of glory with Christ.

It is Christ who provides the key to God's plan. Without him, there is no salvation, and the Christian is nothing. It is only as we are identified with him that we can hope to share in his victory over death, and in the eternal home he has planned for us. The future glory begins now – in faithful service and obedience.

Postscript *The biblical emphasis regarding God's sovereignty and man's free-will is not found somewhere between the two, but in both extremes. If we over-emphasise man's free-will then God will seem to be powerless. If we over-emphasise God's sovereignty then man will seem to be denied any choice.*

Specific Matthew 22:14 Romans 9:20,21,27
Separated Romans 8:29 Ephesians 1:4 1 Peter 1:1,2
Called Philippians 2:12,13 Acts 9:15 1 Peter 2:9-12
Preparing 2 Thessalonians 2:13,14 Revelation 17:14

THOUGHT STARTERS

1 Read Ephesians 1:3-12. Which verses refer to God's call from eternity? What should be the reaction of those who are called? What is the immediate purpose of this call, the future purpose and the ultimate purpose?

2 Meditate on those scriptures where God's sovereignty and man's free-will are combined. For example, John 6:37,44; 2 Peter 1:10,11

3 Why should a true understanding of predestination not stop us from urging those we know to choose to become Christians?

4 Some may argue that they are not called. Where does Scripture teach that God's redemption is offered to *all?* Compare your findings with, for example, 1 Timothy 2:4,6; Titus 2:11.

Boat building in India. 'We are God's workmanship, created in Christ Jesus to do good works' (Ephesians 2:10).

MAN'S NEED OF SALVATION

The Key Truth   *Man is estranged and cut off from God. He needs a new direction and nature, if he is to avoid permanent ruin and eternal judgement. He cannot bring about this change for himself.*

Man's need of a new direction

Although created by God, and for him, mankind has left the path of obedience to God. We are out of touch with God and all that he has planned for us, and without him life does not make sense to us.

Mankind is also under judgement. Jesus Christ's analysis was that the majority of humanity is treading the path of ruin and destruction. People are condemned for their rejection of God's truth.

Man's need of a new nature

Man is in bondage to himself because of his refusal to follow God's commands. On our own, we are unable to change our nature as the sin principle dominates us, and our actions and habits show that we are in slavery.

Man lives his life under the shadow of death, and over the ages no amount of philosophy, guesswork or moral endeavour has been able to remove the spectre of ageing and dying.

Man's need of a new motivation

The brevity and purposelessness of life without God are reflected in art and literature throughout history, particularly in times when society openly rejects God's standards.

The Bible indicates that we need the dimension of God if life is to be lived with dynamism and purpose. Man without God finds no satisfying, alternative way of life.

BIBLE CHECK

Direction   Hebrews 9:27   Matthew 7:13   John 3:19
Nature   Jeremiah 13:23; 17:9,10   John 8:34   Ecclesiastes 8:8

Man's need of personal fulfilment

Man is in urgent need of a sense of destiny and achievement in this world. His aspirations will sometimes take the form of extreme materialistic ambitions; at other times they will shrivel into despair and aimlessness.

Jesus warned his hearers that a person's life should never be totally taken up with the accumulation of possessions. He taught that whoever spent his life and energies upon the material world would have made a bad bargain.

Man's need of social acceptance

From earliest times, as illustrated by the story of the Tower of Babel, mankind has been aware of the need for the friendship and acceptance of others. History illustrates his search for true fellowship, mutual trust and brotherhood.

But ideals, agreements and political arrangements all fall short of what he searches for. The cynicism expressed in the book of Ecclesiastes shows us this clearly. Man is a lonely being.

Man's need of a spiritual dimension

Man as he is cannot appreciate the spiritual side of life. But because God made him, he feels incomplete without a Godward dimension.

Furthermore, he is unable to explore this dimension unaided, because he is described as being poor, weak, blind, and even dead. In the absence of spiritual awareness, his prospects appear to make a mockery of his once high position.

Postscript *Although man does need God's salvation, many people are unaware of their own need. A person may become so used to living in separation from God, that conscience becomes dead. Such complacence is only further proof of the ruined nature of man.*

Motivation Ecclesiastes 6:12 John 6:66-68
Fulfilment Ecclesiastes 2:10,11 Luke 12:15 Mark 8:34-37
Acceptance Genesis 11:4 Ecclesiastes 5:8
Dimension 1 Corinthians 2:14 2 Corinthians 4:4

THOUGHT STARTERS

1 Study Ecclesiastes 2:1-11. Try to analyse this profile of man without God. What drives him? What is his programme? What are his achievements and what does he get? Has verse 11 found an echo in other generations?

2 How far are people in your own fellowship beginning to experience the answers of God to all these needs in man?

3 What makes Ecclesiastes so relevant to much of twentieth-century society?

4 How far have you experienced these needs in your own life? How far do you still experience them?

A wreck off the Southern English coast. 'For the Son of Man came to seek and to save what was lost' (Luke 19:10).

THE WAY OF SALVATION

The Key Truth   *In all the preaching of the early church, as documented in the book of Acts, the way of salvation follows a distinctive pattern. First there is the basis of salvation – Christ's death and resurrection – followed by God's call; and then there is the promise to all who respond.*

The basis – the death of Jesus

The apostles proclaimed the death of Jesus Christ as the means by which God has dealt with the sins of mankind. They declared that without his death there could be no basis for salvation. On the cross, Christ accepted the judgement and separation from God brought about by the sins of the world.

This message directly fulfilled Old Testament prophecy, and the words of Christ himself. It was also taught in the New Testament letters.

The basis – the resurrection of Jesus

If the cross was seen as the means by which God had dealt with sin, the resurrection was proclaimed by the early church as the evidence and proof that Christ's death had been truly effective, and had been recognised by God the Father.

The message of Christ's resurrection was not taught merely as a point of academic discussion. The early witnesses announced it as a living reality.

The call – to repentance

The good news was recognised to have a distinctive moral challenge at its heart. The sinner who hears the gospel is called upon to 'repent', which means to turn from the old life. This turning is more than a mere regret for the past. It is a change of attitude, leading to a change of direction.

BIBLE CHECK

Death   Acts 4:10-12   Isaiah 53:4-6   1 Peter 3:18
Resurrection   Acts 2:32-36   Romans 8:11

The call – to faith

If repentance is seen as a *turning* from the old life, faith is to be understood in similarly active terms. It is turning towards the saving power of Jesus Christ.

There are three aspects to faith. There is *belief in a fact*, for true faith must start by believing with the mind. There is also *belief in a word*, or promise – particularly as given by God. But, vitally, there is *belief in a person* – Jesus Christ. This requires a living relationship of love and trust with Christ. Without these three aspects faith is incomplete.

The promise – forgiveness

There is a finality and a completeness about the forgiveness of sins that is promised to all who respond to the good news of Christ.

Forgiveness is made available only at the price of Christ's death, and God gives it freely and permanently. To be forgiven does not merely mean the wiping away of our past sins – it means the beginning of a new way of life. Because God forgives us, we are able to enjoy his friendship and acceptance.

The promise – the gift of the Spirit

The forgiveness of sins and the gift of the Spirit go together as the promise of New Testament Christianity. God freely gives us the Holy Spirit when we repent and believe in him.

The gift of the Spirit makes the blessings of the gospel and the presence of Christ personal to the Christian. He gives us power for service and reassures us of the promise of eternal life. The Holy Spirit makes *actual* all that Christ's death made *available*.

Postscript *In becoming a Christian there is a part that only we can play and a part that only God can play. We repent and abandon our old way of life. God forgives us and empowers us through the Holy Spirit.*

Repentance Acts 3:19 Luke 15:10; 24:46,47
Faith Acts 13:38,39; 26:18 John 3:16 Revelation 3:20
Forgiveness Acts 3:19 Psalm 103:11,12 Ephesians 1:7,8
Gift of Spirit Acts 2:38 Ephesians 1:13,14

THOUGHT STARTERS

1 Start reading half way through Paul's sermon in Acts 13:22-41. What are the main elements in Paul's message? What is said about Jesus, and how is it said?

2 Try to isolate one or more New Testament passages that helpfully sum up the message of salvation. Compare your findings with others. For instance, look at John 3, Romans 3, Ephesians 2, Titus 3.

3 What is the relative importance of the mind, the emotions and the will in the response of the individual to the good news?

4 What is the main goal in proclaiming salvation in Christ? Check your thoughts against Colossians 1:28, and Matthew 28:19,20.

South Stack Lighthouse, Anglesey. 'I am the light of the world. Whoever follows me will never walk in darkness, but will have the light of life' (John 8:12).

ACCEPTANCE

The Key Truth *The sinner is accepted by God in Christ, and made a new person. The benefits this position and relationship bring should make the Christian eternally grateful.*

God regenerates the believer as a new being

So radical is the renewing work of the Spirit, that it is spoken of in terms of new birth, or 'regeneration'. It is described as birth 'from above'. As an individual repents and believes in Christ, so the Holy Spirit enters his life and personality and joins him to the family of God. The Spirit also gives him a new nature – characterised by the hallmarks of a new moral outlook, love for the family of God, and faith in Christ.

God reconciles the believer in a new relationship

Until the good news is received and acted upon, a state of hostility exists between God and the individual. It is the death of Christ that specifically alters the situation. On the cross, Christ himself accepted the guilt and penalty for the sins of mankind. The way is opened for a repentant sinner to receive the reconciliation thus made available by God in Christ.

It is the cross that satisfies God's justice – for there sin's punishment is fully paid. It is also the cross that satisfies God's mercy, for there sin is fully forgiven. A state of friendship begins between God and the new Christian.

God redeems the believer through a new covenant

The old covenant was an agreement entered into by God with the Jews, primarily on the basis of the law of

---

BIBLE CHECK

Regenerates Ezekiel 36:25-27   John 3:3-8   Titus 3:4,5
Reconciles 2 Corinthians 5:18-21   Romans 5:10

Moses. It established a way of life for them after their deliverance from Egypt.

The new covenant (foretold by Jeremiah) was to achieve through the cross what the old could never do. The deliverance was of another kind; personal and internal, on the basis of Christ's shed blood, for the forgiveness of sins and the redeeming (or 'buying back') of the sinner. This was a costly price indeed.

God justifies the believer for a new position

To 'justify' is a legal term, which means to declare that a person is innocent. God has done this for the person who has responded to Christ, on the basis of the death of Jesus.

Justification is said to be *by 'grace'* (which means God's undeserved favour), for it is a free gift. It is also *by blood,* for Christ's death is the means by which God could legally forgive the sinner. It is also *by faith,* for there is nothing the sinner can contribute to his new position of righteousness – nothing beyond accepting the gift in grateful faith.

God glorifies the believer for a new life

In the New Testament letters, it is noticeable that salvation is repeatedly expressed in three stages. First, there is the free *grace* of God as the initial act and base. Second, there is the growth of *godliness* in the Christian as a progressive experience. Third, *glory* is seen as the future goal and pinnacle. The Christian's great confidence is in the certain return of Christ, the promise of a resurrection body and a share in God's eternal glory.

Postscript   *New believers may be confident that God has accepted them because of the promises in the* word *of God, the finished* work *of Christ and the inward* witness *of the Holy Spirit.*

Redeems Jeremiah 31:31-34   Mark 14:24   1 Peter 1:18,19
Justifies Romans 3:23-26; 5:1   Titus 3:7
Glorifies Romans 8:28-30   Philippians 3:20,21

THOUGHT STARTERS

1 Read Romans 5:1-11, with its portrait of the Christian's new position in Christ. Look for the key terms. List the ways in which God has been generous to us, and give thanks to him for them.

2 In what sense can we say that we have been 'justified by grace/blood/faith'?

3 Write down the qualities you have enjoyed in a relationship with one of your friends. Write down the demands such a relationship makes. How is your relationship with God the same, and how is it different?

4 Do the Christian's troubles end, upon entering into peace with God? What does Romans 5:1-5 teach us?

Ruin, cross and lighthouse, Anglesey. 'For the wages of sin is death, but the gift of God is eternal life' (Romans 6:23).

SANCTIFICATION

The Key Truth   *The word 'sanctification' describes the process that God wants every Christian to experience. God wants us to be sanctified, increasingly to become more like him in all that we think and do. Sanctification means to grow in holiness.*

A separation to God

While justification is the work of a moment – that of *declaring* the sinner righteous – Sanctification is the process of a lifetime – that of *making* the sinner righteous in life and character.

Holiness means separateness. In the Old Testament, houses and animals were sometimes set apart for the special use of God. Christ's followers have been called by God to be set apart – so that they may become more like Christ and holy in character.

A separation from the world

The Christian is called to co-operate with the sanctifying purposes and power of God. There must be a willingness to abandon evil and impure ways; to be separate from all that could impede the development of Christ-like living.

Sanctification is not the separation of a hermit or recluse, because Jesus mixed with sinners and yet in his standards and character was 'set apart' from sinners (Hebrews 7:26). His desire for his followers is that they remain involved in the world, while remaining free from its evil.

A separation for holy living

Success in Christian living is, to a great degree, dependent on our readiness to be given to God in total self-sacrifice and surrender.

BIBLE CHECK

To God Leviticus 27:14 2 Thessalonians 2:13
From the World 2 Corinthians 6:17-7:1 John 17:15

The Christian who takes holiness seriously is viewed as a 'slave' of righteousness; as a 'living sacrifice' to God; as a clean household utensil.

A separation by the Holy Spirit

Although the Christian's co-operation is vital in the process of sanctification, the power comes from the Holy Spirit.

In Old Testament times, some of God's people longed for the time when God would change them from within, giving them the *desire* as well as the *command* to be holy. This is what the Holy Spirit does in us. He gives us right desires and begins to change our characters so that we act in a way that pleases God.

A separation through the word of God

The Bible has a cleansing effect in the Christian's life. The Holy Spirit uses the Bible to enlarge the Christian's vision of Christ and strengthen his desire for holy living.

The Bible is also a guide to the way of life God wants us to live. It shows us what our priorities and attitudes should be. The Bible tells us that the words of God can be planted in our personalities. The Holy Spirit does this.

A separation that progresses throughout life

Sanctification is a process in which encouragement and challenge go side by side. The believer understands that we *have been saved* from the penalty of sin; that we *are being saved* from the power of sin that we *shall be saved* from the presence of sin.

Postscript *The fact that Christians become awake to their sins and failures is a sign of progress. We must go further, however, bringing our sins to God for his forgiveness, and enlarging our vision of Christ. In this way we shall increasingly want to be more like him. It is in the area of motives that the battle for holiness rages the strongest.*

Holy Living Romans 6:19; 12:1 2 Timothy 2:20,21
Holy Spirit Ezekiel 36:27 Galatians 5:16-18
Word of God John 15:3; 17:17 Psalm 119:9 James 1:21
Life 2 Corinthians 1:10; 3:18 1 Thessalonians 5:23

THOUGHT STARTERS

1 Read 2 Peter 1:3-11. How are the Christian readers of this letter described, as regards their past state, their present responsibilities and their future goals?

2 Forgiveness is always free. But to presume on God's mercy, in order to continue in sin, has no place in the Christian life. Why? Compare your answer with Titus 2:11-14.

3 What are the tensions of staying involved in the world, and yet being separate from its evil (John 17:15)?

4 Effort seems to be required of Christians who desire to grow (2 Peter 1:5-7,10). What kind of effort is needed? What are the rewards for such efforts, as mentioned in the passage?

Bridges open for ships, Chicago. 'The righteousness of the blameless makes a straight way for them . . .' (Proverbs 11:5).

IN THE LETTER TO THE ROMANS

The Key Truth   *The letter to the Romans is the apostle Paul's 'Manifesto' of Christian truth, in which the way of salvation is clearly proclaimed and applied.*

IT FEATURES THE FOLLOWING THEMES

Condemnation – Romans 1:1-3:20
Paul tells us that the theme of his letter is 'the righteousness of God'. He then shows that the righteousness of the Gentile and Jewish world falls far short of God's standard and is therefore under his condemnation. All the world is guilty.

Justification – Romans 3:20-4:25
God's way of declaring the sinner to be righteous is independent of Old Testament law (although the Old Testament witnesses to it). It is provided freely, through the death of Christ, for all who have faith of the kind illustrated in Abraham.

Reconciliation – Romans 5:1-21
From the firm base of being put right with God, Paul amplifies the blessings and security of justification for the believer. He contrasts Adam with Christ – the new representative and Head of the human race, whose one righteous act is capable of setting free all mankind.

Identification – Romans 6:1-23
Paul defends the truth of justification against the charge that it encourages deliberate continuation in sin and in lawlessness. Paul argues that the believer has now been identified with Christ in his death and resurrection, and indeed has become a 'slave' of righteousness.

BIBLE CHECK

Condemnation   Romans 3:9,19   **Justification**   Romans 3:24,25   **Reconciliation**   Romans 5:10,11   **Identification**

Liberation – Romans 7:1-25

From Justification and Identification with Christ, Paul moves to a third privilege of the believer – freedom from slavery to the law. The Christian's slavery is now to Christ in the new way of the Spirit (verses 1-6). It is not the law, of course, that is to be blamed for man's sin, but fallen human nature (verses 7-13). In his internal conflict, the Christian may know liberation and power (verses 14-25).

Sanctification – Romans 8:1-39

Now that the old legal slavery belongs to the past, those who belong to Christ live by a stronger principle and power – the life of the Spirit. Those whose life is controlled by the Holy Spirit fulfil God's laws from the heart. They are assured by the Spirit's presence in their lives that they are God's children. Nothing can now separate them from the love of Christ.

Election – Romans 9:1-11:36

Paul now faces the problem of the Jew's rejection of their own Messiah. He interprets this in the light of *election* – the truth that God chooses a people for himself. God is supremely sovereign, and uses even the disobedience of the Jews to divert his blessing to the rest of the world. Meanwhile God still has a future for the Jews.

Transformation – Romans 12:1-15:13

Paul applies himself to the practical duties of Christian living. The life of the believer is to be a transformed life of service, sharing with other Christians, duty to the government, and respect for others' convictions.

Postscript *All who have encountered salvation will want to know more about the truth of their experience. Although the book of Romans may tax the reader's concentration, it is rewarding to read through it slowly and understand the truth of salvation at a deeper level.*

Romans 6:6	**Liberation**	Romans 7:6	**Sanctification**
Romans 8:11	**Election**	Romans 9:21-24	**Transformation**
Romans 12:1,2			

THOUGHT STARTERS

1 Read Romans 8:28-39. In what way is God's purpose working on behalf of his people? What great themes of the letter to the Romans can you trace in this passage?

2 In verses 31-39, what reasons does the apostle give for his triumphant confidence – in terms of the believer's relationship to God, to Christ, and to circumstances?

3 Look at the question of verse 31. What do the themes of Romans mean to you, or what are they beginning to mean to you?

4 A review question: in what way are justification and sanctification different from each other?

Golden Gate Bridge, San Francisco. 'There is one God and one mediator between God and men, the man Christ Jesus' (1 Timothy 2:5).

The
Christian

DESCRIBED

The Key Truth *A Christian is a person who has received Jesus Christ as Saviour and Lord, and has submitted to the rule of God's kingdom.*

A sinner saved by grace

It was at Antioch that believers in Christ were first called *Christians* – probably as a term of abuse. However, Christians have always valued this identification, because of the immensity of the debt they owe to Christ, after whom they are called.

It is God's grace that has brought the sinner into union with Christ. Grace is the free, unearned favour of God towards the sinner. This grace is only possible because of the cross, and it is made real to us by the Holy Spirit. Salvation cannot be earned. It is a free gift to be received by faith.

A member of God's family

In his letter to the Roman Christians, the apostle Paul teaches that the people who did not belong to God at all are now, by his grace, called sons of the living God.

Such a title is not naturally ours. It is only given to those who receive Jesus Christ. It is by the power of God's love that this 'adoption' into his family takes place. Being part of the church means to learn the discipline and joy of being in the family.

A disciple of Jesus Christ

A 'disciple' in Jesus' day was a person who followed both his master's teaching and his way of life. Christ said that those who were willing to love *him* and obey him first above all else were his disciples. A Christian is a person who has responded to his call, 'follow me'.

BIBLE CHECK

Sinner Acts 11:26 Ephesians 2:8,9 1 Timothy 1:15
Member Romans 9:25,26 John 1:12,13 Ephesians 3:14,15

A temple of the Holy Spirit

In the Old Testament, the Jews were given special instructions on how to build the temple – and on it they lavished all their riches, craftsmanship and care, so that God should be glorified in every possible way. In his letter to the Corinthians, Paul tells us that our bodies are the temple of the Holy Spirit. This means that all our abilities and powers should be devoted towards glorifying God.

A pilgrim in an alien environment

Many of the Old Testament's great figures are described as people who had no permanent home of their own. Abraham, for example, left the security of his family home to live in tents in a foreign land. The writer to the Hebrews describes such people as those who saw that the earth was not their home. Similarly, the New Testament urges us not to put our trust in material possessions, and to guard against indiscipline. For we too must realise that this earth is not our true home. Christians are like foreigners and strangers, with their permanent home elsewhere.

A citizen of heaven

The Christian will not find permanence in this earthly existence; the permanent city still lies in the future. But the full membership and many of the privileges of that better city are with every Christian now.

As a result, the Christian is described as a citizen of heaven. We see ourselves as people who belong to another country – and we are ambassadors of that country while we live on earth.

Postscript *It is unwise, and untrue to the Bible, to believe that a person can receive Jesus Christ as Saviour without receiving him as Lord.*

Disciple Luke 14:26,27 Matthew 9:9
Temple 1 Kings 6 Acts 7:48,49 1 Corinthians 6:19,20
Pilgrim Exodus 22:21 Hebrews 11:8-16 1 Peter 2:11,12
Citizen Ephesians 2:19 Hebrews 13:14 Revelation 22:14

THOUGHT STARTERS

1 Study Ephesians 2:1-10,19. Reflect on the 'but' of verse 4. In what way is it the shaft of light that illuminates the passage? If you were going to speak on verses 8 and 9, what major points would you make?

2 Two descriptions of the Christian are given in Ephesians 2:19. To what extent have you experienced the privileges implied by these terms?

3 What are the insecure aspects of being a Christian? What are the secure aspects?

4 Try to think of some less prominent biblical illustrations of the Christian, and of what they imply. (Clue: look at 2 Timothy 2.)

Switzerland. Climber on the snow. '. . . doing the will of God from your heart' (Ephesians 6:6).

THE CHRISTIAN AND THE BIBLE

The Key Truth   *Through the Bible, the Christian comes to an understanding of God's plan, and receives nourishment for Christian living.*

THE BIBLE

Directs the Christian for life

Biblically, a disciple of Jesus is recognised by unashamed loyalty to Christ's person and unquestioning obedience to his commands. The Master cannot accept disciples who want to establish their own method of instruction or set their own course.

Jesus taught that those obedient to his words would be characterised by stability; the disobedient would be overthrown. This is a principle throughout scripture. *The Bible is like a lamp, guiding the Christian.*

Equips the Christian for battle

The believer must learn from Christ, who resisted the Devil's temptations in the wilderness with his knowledge of the Old Testament. A working knowledge of the Bible is a weapon of spiritual power.

Equally, in defending the Christian faith, the Christian who enters the arena having thought through the issues beforehand is at an immense advantage. A biblically-trained mind is a weapon of priceless value. *The Bible is like a sword, protecting the Christian.*

Energises the Christian for service

The disciple is called to be fruitful in service, bringing both the compassion and challenge of Christ's message to bear upon a needy world.

It is the inexhaustible supply found in God's living word that gives Christian service its vitality and fresh-

BIBLE CHECK

Directs   John 8:31,32   Matthew 7:24-27   Psalm 119:105
Equips   Matthew 4:1-11   1 Timothy 1:18,19   Ephesians 6:17
Energises   John 15:16   Isaiah 55:10,11   Psalm 1

ness. The Bible's depths can never be plumbed. *The Bible is like water, renewing the Christian.*

Corrects the Christian from error

The Bible exposes and corrects many errors and distortions of true belief. There is the *legalist* – the victim of convention; the empty *ritualist* – the victim of superstition; the *tranditionalist* – the victim of pride; the *rationalist* – the victim of unbelief; and the mere *theorist* – the victim of laziness.

The Bible is God's message to us. Because of this, we should always be open to it to correct our own wrong ideas, and to replace them with God's truth. *The Bible is like a mirror, reforming the Christian.*

Develops the Christian in the faith

The Bible is food for every Christian. We are called upon to grow up from spiritual childhood, strengthened by God's word.

As we advance towards maturity, we should be able to see the great themes of scripture as a connected whole, rather than as a collection of scattered thoughts. *The Bible is like milk, nourishing the Christian.*

Informs the Christian of God's mind

The Bible is God's written revelation. It is impossible to arrive at a knowledge of his plan and will on the strength of our own guesswork. God has given us the Bible so that we should not be in the dark about who he is, and what he is doing.

The true wisdom that leads to salvation is arrived at by a humble and careful study of God's word. *The Bible is like treasure, enriching the believer.*

Postscript   *To develop a balanced faith, the Christian should read the Bible regularly and thoroughly. Unless we read all of the Bible, we may distort or over-emphasise some aspect of its message.*

Corrects Isaiah 29:13   Mark 7:9-13   James 1:23-25
Develops 2 Timothy 2:15   1 Corinthians 14:20   1 Peter 2:2,3
Informs Romans 11:33-36   2 Timothy 3:14,15   Psalm 119,162

THOUGHT STARTERS

1 Read 2 Timothy 3:14-4:5. What is the nature of the Bible's power, and what does it achieve? What can regular readers expect it to do in their lives? What are the dangers which may be avoided through the Bible's message?

2 What would be a good plan and schedule for the reading of the Bible? What plans have your friends found helpful?

3 Why is it vital to become mature in the truth of the Bible? Compare your findings with Acts 20:29-32.

4 Read Psalm 19:7-11. Try to list the ways in which the writer of this Psalm delights in God's word, and make the passage a subject for praising God.

Caernarvon Castle, North Wales. 'You are my refuge and my shield; I have put my hope in your word' (Psalm 119:114).

THE CHRISTIAN AND PRAYER

The Key Truth *Prayer is God's chosen way of communication and fellowship between the Christian and himself. It is the secret of spiritual growth and effective service.*

PRAYER IS ESSENTIAL

For communion with God

Christian prayer is not a technique. To try to manipulate God for our own purposes is the way of magic, and of the old cultic religions – when man is at the centre. With Christian prayer God is at the centre.

On the human level, we do not like to use those whom we love – and the same is true of those who have entered into a relationship with God of trust and acceptance. Jesus taught his friends to talk to God as to their heavenly Father, and not to use meaningless incantations characteristic of heathen worship. For prayer involves a relationship. We should learn from the example of Jesus, who would regularly go away and spend time alone with his Father.

For growth in God

Prayer is like breathing, in the life of a Christian. When we pray regularly, there takes place in our lives a steady growth in character and inner resources. Contrary to popular opinion, prayer is not a sign of weakness, but of strength and progress.

Prayer is an education. The disciples needed to be taught by Jesus, and he gave them a pattern of prayer that the church has never forgotten. The Christian of every age faces the same lessons, disciplines and privileges of growing in God.

For the service of God

God does not need our prayers. Prayer does not affect

BIBLE CHECK

Communion   Matthew 6:5-8   Mark 1:35   Luke 5:15,16
Growth   Ephesians 3:14-19   Matthew 6:9-13

his will and overall purpose for us. But the Bible teaches, and our Christian experience confirms, that prayer does affect his specific actions in fulfilling his will.

The reason is that God has appointed prayer as a key way of *involving* his people in the carrying out of his will and service in this world. The Christian learns to pray in the name of Jesus – that is, with his interests at heart. He also learns to pray with the help of the Holy Spirit. Prayer is the most important form of service we can ever employ.

For the praise of God

The Christian is a temple of the Holy Spirit, and is therefore to glorify God in everything. Thanksgiving, joy and praise are key aspects in a Christian's attitude, according to the New Testament.

To praise God is to make great affirmations about him. This is evident in the book of Psalms, in which we repeatedly read of God's greatness and of what he has done for his people. As we meditate on the great themes of the Bible, so our praise of God becomes a vital part of prayer.

For the experience of God

Prayer can bring God into the heart of every human emotion and experience. The writers of the Psalms were able to look to God for guidance in times of uncertainty. The apostles were able to turn to him in praise and prayer when in prison. Paul was strengthened by God, even though his prayer for relief from affliction was not granted. Prayer allows God to mould and develop the new man in Jesus Christ.

Postscript   *There is a particular power and the promised presence of Christ when believers meet together to pray in his name – according to the promise of Matthew 18:19,20.*

Service James 5:16-18   Ephesians 6:18
Praise 1 Thessalonians 5:16-18   Psalm 34:1-3   Psalm 150
Experience Psalm 57:1-3   Acts 16:22-25   2 Corinthians 12:7-10

THOUGHT STARTERS

1 Think about the Lord's prayer as recorded in Matthew 6:9-13. What pattern does it set for us in our prayer life? What similar patterns have you established in your own praying?

2 Why bother to pray? Try to list some convincing reasons.

3 Why do most people find prayer not the easiest of activities? How can we help one another in this?

4 A Scottish preacher has said, 'We have actually got it all wrong when we speak as we do about "praying for the work", because prayer *is* the work.' How do you react to this statement?

Oaku, Hawaii. 'And the peace of God . . . will guard your hearts and your minds in Christ Jesus' (Philippians 4:7).

THE CHRISTIAN AND WITNESS

The Key Truth *Christian witness is the means by which God, through his servants, continues the work of his Son, in bringing the message of salvation to the world.*

Proclaiming a person

Because Christianity is concerned with a person rather than with a philosophy or religious system, the early disciples of Christ found little difficulty in witnessing. Whatever their education or background, they had all experienced the transforming power of the risen Christ.

Their witness was about him – and so Philip on the desert road spoke of *Jesus* to the Ethiopian official. This means that all who obey Jesus as Lord have something to share. Every Christian is a witness.

Explaining the truth

While it is Christ we proclaim, there are, however, important facts in the Christian message which must be explained and understood if individuals are to become more than mere converts. The apostle Paul's aim was that men and women should grow to become spiritually mature in Christ.

In societies where there is little awareness of God or the Bible, it is vital that the truth should be taught argued and explained.

Sharing a love

Behind the message of reconciliation is the motivating power of Christ's love. Christ sends us out into the world not merely to talk about him, but to share his love and our love with others. Paul said that he preached because he was compelled by the love of Christ.

BIBLE CHECK

Person Acts 1:8; 8:35 Luke 24:46-48
Truth Colossians 1:28,29 Acts 18:4 2 Timothy 2:2
Love 2 Corinthians 5:14 1 Thessalonians 2:7-13

Witnessing consistently

Jesus said that the mark of his disciples was to be the presence of love in their fellowship. Their lives were to shine as lights in the world, through their words, their deeds and their life-style.

Such a witness is not a burdened, strained obligation. It springs naturally out of the life lived in union with Christ. Such witness is ready to seize and buy up the opportunities as they come; to give answers to those who are seeking, with humility and love.

Witnessing personally

When the early church experienced its first persecution, the believers were scattered throughout Judea and Samaria – all except for the apostles. Although these Christians were without the leadership of the apostles, we learn that they went everywhere, witnessing of Christ.

It was a matter of standing out in unashamed and personal testimony. Earlier the apostles had declared that it was impossible for them to keep silent about Christ. When we are living close to the love of God, we find that we cannot keep the good news to ourselves.

Witnessing collectively

There is great strength and encouragement for all who join in combined witness. Jesus recognised the need to send his disciples out two by two. On the day of Pentecost, as Peter rose to proclaim Christ, his eleven companions stood with him. The book of Acts repeatedly tells us that the first Christians worked together.

Here was a unity in proclamation – a characteristic of any church which is working *with* Christ.

Postscript *Witnessing should never be a burdensome Christian duty, but the grateful privilege of those who have an experience of Jesus Christ.*

Consistently John 13:34,35 Philippians 2:14-16 1 Peter 3:15
Personally Acts 8:1,4 Acts 4:18-20 Psalm 40:10
Collectively Acts 2:14,42-47 Philippians 1:27

THOUGHT STARTERS

1 Read the story of Philip and the Ethiopian official in Acts 8:26-40. What can we learn from Philip about bringing others to Jesus Christ? What qualities do we see in Philip? How prepared was the official for this encounter?

2 Which is easier – to speak to a stranger or to an acquaintance about Christ? Which seems to be more effective, and why?

3 Read 1 Thessalonians 2:7-13. List the qualities of Paul in this passage – his motive, his efforts, his persistence. How should these verses affect our way of spreading the good news?

4 Bearing in mind your gifts, what is there that you can do, naturally and freely, to help make Christ better known?

Lightship on the Solent, England. 'Let your light shine before men, that they may see your good deeds and praise your Father in heaven' (Matthew 5:16).

THE CHRISTIAN AND THE WORLD

The Key Truth   *The Christian has been called out of the world to be holy, but also he has been sent into the world for service and evangelism.*

THE CHRISTIAN IS

Called out of the world

'The world' means both this present, temporary *age*, and the hostile *system* of thought and action that operates on this planet. This is our environment.

But the Christian's true home is not here. Whatever our physical situation – good or bad – all that we value most strongly (our heavenly Father, Jesus Christ, our inheritance, our hope) is elsewhere. The New Testament urges Christ's followers to set their hearts on the eternal and heavenly dimension.

Separated from the world

This thread runs through most of the New Testament letters. Christians, because of their heavenward calling, are to avoid the trends and evil associations of fallen society. Their ethical standards are to be the highest of all.

Separation, however, does not mean that the Christian is called to withdraw from society, but to be kept committed to Christ within it.

Sent into the world

The appeal of the New Testament is not simply that Christ's disciples should avoid being polluted by the world; rather they are to purify it. The Christian's attitude to the world should never be one of contempt. It is God's world, and we are to be involved in its redemption.

BIBLE CHECK

Called   1 Corinthians 7:29-31   Hebrews 10:33,34
Colossians 3:1,2
Separated   James 4:4,5   Ephesians 5:3-11   John 17:15,16

To overcome the world

We must avoid judgemental views that simply dismiss the world as beyond the reach and care of God. But on the other hand, we should not fall into the trap of believing that the world is morally, socially or politically perfectible, however much may be done by Christians and others of good will to alleviate its problems. The true redemption of the world cannot be completed until the future glory of Christ is revealed.

Thus, the Christian is called upon to overcome the evil tendencies and pressures that the world brings to bear upon him. We are caught in a spiritual battle that involves every Christian in this dark age, and therefore we must be armed with spiritual weapons. Christ himself has given us the assurance of his strength for the fight, and of the ultimate victory of God over all evil.

To journey through the world

The Christian is a citizen of heaven, with relationships and privileges that are outside this world. We are like the Old Testament Jews, journeying towards a promised land, confident in the assurance of God's presence and guidance.

The pilgrim is required to exercise obedience and discipline. At times we are likened to a soldier who cannot afford to get entangled in civilian pursuits – or to an athlete who must observe the necessary rules. Our Christian life is the story of a pilgrimage through a world that is staggering under its problems. But we travel on with faith as our lamp.

Postscript *A true understanding of the world that God loves will strengthen the Christian's calling to go into all the world and proclaim Christ to every person.*

Sent John 20:21 Matthew 5:13-16 John 3:16,17
Overcome Romans 8:19-21 Ephesians 6:10-18
Romans 8:37
Journey Philippians 3:20 Joshua 1:9 Hebrews 11:16

THOUGHT STARTERS

1 Read and study 2 Timothy 4:1-22. Paul is in prison, nearing the end of his pilgrimage, in Rome. How does he view the current scene, his own situation and future, and his acquaintances? Contrast the careers of Demas and Mark (compare with Acts 15:37-39).

2 The Christian does not regard the present world system as perfectible. How can we avoid adopting either a judgemental attitude that writes the world off, or an extreme optimism that ends in disillusionment?

3 Read John 16:33. Why did Jesus encourage his disciples by saying these words? What do they mean for them – and us?

4 How can we keep our eternal goals clearly in view?

New York City and the Hudson River at night. 'Do not love the world or anything in the world' (1 John 2:15).

THE CHRISTIAN LIFE

The Key Truth *A Christian is a new being in Christ, reaching full potential as progress in life and faith is made. The Christian life is seen in these ways:*

A vocation to be fulfilled

The New Testament overflows with phrases that speak of goals, aims and ambitions. The apostle Paul alone is an example. He wants to finish his course; he desires to win the approval of God; he longs to proclaim Christ to those who have never heard of him. All his ambitions were centred in Christ himself, who was to have first place in everything.

All Christians have a calling – to be God's own people. Such a vocation overrides all other callings in life and, indeed, enhances them.

A character to be developed

God's purpose for his people is that they should become like his Son Jesus Christ in the holiness of their living. To be a Christian does not mean only to believe in certain facts about Christ. Rather, it means to develop a Christ-like character. The Christian is to co-operate in this process, combating sinful habits and attitudes through the power of the Holy Spirit.

A fellowship to be maintained

The Christian is given ways and means by which the relationship with Christ may be maintained. Two examples of this are prayer and the Lord's supper.

The apostle John's first letter has much to say about the fellowship of the Christian life. It is a fellowship of *life,* for it centres in Christ, the Word of life. It is a fellowship of *love,* for all who are connected to Christ are connected also to each other. It is a fellowship of

BIBLE CHECK

Vocation Philippians 3:14   Romans 15:20   Colossians 1:18
Character Romans 8:29   2 Peter 1:5-8   Ephesians 5:1,2
Fellowship 1 John 1:1-7   Ephesians 4:3-6   John 15:4

light, for there can be no darkness or hidden impurity where God is involved.

Energies to be harnessed

God has given us many natural gifts. When we become Christians we are not to give up these abilities. Instead, motivated by the truths of our faith, we are to devote them to God's use, that they may reach their full potential and power.

The quality of daily work, our relationships and service will be heightened by the dynamic of Christ's resurrection power. We should recognise that we are not placed on this earth simply for ourselves. We are to be used.

Minds to be developed

A Christian framework of thinking enables an individual to establish his relationship to the universe – simply because Christianity is true. By opening our intellects to the truth of God, we can be convinced about the deepest issues of life.

Each Christian must see to it that his mind is stretched to the limits of its capacity. Paul described those who were swept about with every shifting belief as 'babies'. His prayer was that the minds of younger Christians might be illuminated fully by the light of Christ. They were to be adult in their understanding.

A hope to be realised

It is the historic nature of the Christian faith – culminating in the resurrection of Jesus – that gives to God's people the eager expectation of their final inheritance in glory. The one who was raised will surely return; the past is forgiven; the present is covered, and tomorrow belongs to us.

Postscript   *It is vital that Christ's followers should make, not merely converts, but disciples, men and women of mature character and sound judgement.*

Energies   1 Corinthians 15:58   Ephesians 2:10
Colossians 3:23,24
Minds   1 John 5:20   Ephesians 4:13,14   Ephesians 1:18
Hope   1 Peter 1:3-9   Titus 2:13   Revelation 22:20

THOUGHT STARTERS

1 Read John 15:1-17. Reflect on what it means to be united to Jesus Christ. How is this achieved? What are Christ's expectations of his people? What are the privileges and challenges of this relationship?

2 Bertrand Russell (who was an atheist) once said of Christianity: 'There is nothing to be said against it, except that it is too difficult for most of us to practise sincerely.' How accurate is this assessment? Give your reasons.

3 How does your Christian faith affect your daily work? Discuss this with your friends.

4 How would you describe your relationship with Jesus Christ?

Climber in Snowdonia, North Wales. 'The life I live in the body, I live by faith in the Son of God, who loved me and gave himself for me' (Galatians 2:20).

The Church

ITS CHARACTERISTICS

The Key Truth *The church of Christ is the whole company of redeemed people. Christ is present and active in the church, and uses it for his work in the world.*

It is the church of Jesus Christ (historical)

Through the centuries it is only the church that has experienced the presence of Jesus Christ within its membership. This is because it is *Christ's* church, purchased for himself by his own blood, and cared for as a husband cares for his wife. Jesus declared that where two or three individuals meet in his name there his promised presence would be experienced. No matter how small the group – there is the church.

It is the company of all believers (universal)

This is the church of *different eras;* past, present and future – together, they form the church. It is the church of *different cultures,* found in countries scattered over the earth, but united by its common Lord. It is a church of *different characteristics,* abilities and temperaments; and it is a church featuring *different levels of experience,* from elderly Christians to the newest disciples – yet one church.

It is a unity of the Spirit (spiritual)

The unity of the Spirit, of which the apostle Paul wrote, is more important than the differences of groups and denominations. The church can only truly be one, because of the one Spirit who unites it.

Although all Christians are to work for unity and mend divisions, it is not uniformity nor unanimity that they are to seek. Rather, it is a recognition of all who exhibit the family likeness.

Its authority is God's word (scriptural)

Down the ages the church has had a vital relationship

BIBLE CHECK

Historical Matthew 16:18   Matthew 18:20
Universal Colossians 3:11   Revelation 7:9,10

with the scriptures; it is the scriptural revelation that is the basis of the church's belief and stability.

The church has been commissioned to defend this revelation, to proclaim it, and to submit to its authority. The Bible is the church's authority and tells us all that we need to know about salvation and Christian conduct. On these, the Bible has the final say. On other matters, however, such as church government, there is no clear blueprint – and this no doubt helps to explain the differences existing between churches even in New Testament times.

Its programme is world-wide (international)

The programme of the church is the programme of Christ. Jesus said that his task was to bring good news to the poor and liberation to the oppressed.

When Christ's earthly ministry had finished, he commanded the church to carry out his mission to the world. The Book of Acts shows us the way in which the church's mission expanded from Jerusalem to Judea and Samaria, and then to the whole earth. Our task is one of evangelism and service and to do this, we are empowered by the Holy Spirit.

Its destiny is heaven (eternal)

The church on earth is living between two comings. It looks back to the birth and ministry of Jesus Christ, and it looks forward to his glorious return.

Meanwhile it works in the knowledge that Christ is preparing a future home. On a certain day, known only to God, the trumpet will sound, and the church will be united to Christ.

Postscript *The biblical picture of the church, as described above, helps the church to keep the right priorities in its mission and worship. It also serves as an accurate test to show whether movements and sects which claim to be part of the church are true or false.*

Spiritual Ephesians 4:4-6 John 17:20-23
Scriptural Jude 3 2 Timothy 1:13,14
International Luke 4:16-21 John 20:21 Acts 1:8
Eternal Matthew 24:30,31 John 14:1-3

THOUGHT STARTERS

1 Read Ephesians 4:1-16. What gives the church its essential unity (verses 4-6)? How is this preserved? How does this compare with the kind of unity that Christians should seek (verses 11-16). How is this achieved?

2 A church leader once said 'The church is the only institution in the world which exists primarily for the benefit of non-members.' How far do you agree with this statement?

3 Some Christians strongly emphasise their own church tradition. Others treat denominations as unhealthy. Yet others are indifferent. What is your view?

4 Read 1 Timothy 3:15. What can your own circle of Christian friends do to further the truth of God more?

'We are members of his body' (Ephesians 5:30).

ITS MAIN DESCRIPTION

The Key Truth *There are a number of different pictures of the church in the New Testament. Looked at together, these pictures give us a full idea of the nature and character of the church and its mission.*

A firm building

The New Testament letters take up Christ's theme of 'building' his church – although this idea is not to be confused in any way with literal buildings for Christian worship.

The apostles Paul and Peter, in particular, saw the church as a *spiritual building,* composed of 'living stones' – Christians. This picture shows us how Christians depend upon each other and upon Christ as the building's cornerstone.

A virgin bride

A relationship of deep intimacy is suggested by the New Testament idea of the church 'married' to Christ. We are told that Christ loves the church, and has made it pure and faultless by his death.

The apostle John's vision of the new heaven and the new earth describes the church as Christ's bride, prepared and ready to meet her husband.

A functioning body

The picture of the church as a body, with Christ as its head, emphasises that the church is a living organism and not an organisation.

As in the picture of the church as a building, the *dependence* of the church upon Christ is stressed, but we also learn the important truth that no member of the body is disposable – or of overriding importance.

BIBLE CHECK

Building 1 Peter 2:4,5 Ephesians 2:20-22
Bride Ephesians 5:25-27 Revelation 21:2

A permanent city

The theme of the city of God is usually seen in the Bible as a future hope. God's people live as strangers in the world, and are looking for the city which is to come.

The city of God is mentioned a number of times in the Book of Revelation, where the writer is speaking of the church. When God's chosen people are finally brought to completion, the city will be a vast community of purpose, life, activity and permanent security.

A stable family

The terms 'family' or 'household' of God point again to the relationship that exists in the church between the members and the head. And God's very fatherhood provides a pattern for family life now.

Great encouragement – particularly to Gentile converts in the early church – was found in the fact that all shared equally in the privileges of God's household, Jews and Gentiles alike. No longer was the Gentile an outsider or foreigner. This should also be true of the church today – because barriers spoil the family life God wants the church to have.

An active army

The references to the church as an army are not heavily pronounced in scripture. However, the New Testament teaches that the church is involved in a spiritual warfare.

Intensity, activity and victory are the main ideas conveyed to us by this imagery; the weapons and the victory itself being God's.

Postscript *It must be emphasised that the church is an organism rather than an organisation, a living fellowship rather than mere buildings, a close family rather than a collection of individuals.*

Body 1 Corinthians 12:12-31 Ephesians 1:22,23; 4:15,16
City Hebrews 13:14 Revelation 21:10-27
Family Ephesians 2:19; 3:14,15 1 Timothy 3:14,15
Army Ephesians 6:12 Revelation 12:11

THOUGHT STARTERS

1 Read and think about 1 Peter 2:1-10. A number of figurative expressions are used of Christians in this passage. Try to list them, and consider their implications.

2 Which of the various descriptions of the church have you found most helpful? Why?

3 Reflect on how much Christ has done for his church, as you consider each picture of the church in turn.

4 Look at 1 Corinthians 12:12-31. What do these verses tell us about jealousy and pride in the church? How do you regard those in your fellowship who seem more gifted, and those who seem less gifted than yourself?

The rocky coastline of Dorset. 'On this rock I will build my church, and the gates of Hades will not overcome it' (Matthew 16:18).

ITS RELATIONSHIP TO CHRIST

The Key Truth *The life, witness and continuance of the church is totally dependent upon its relationship to Jesus Christ, its builder and protector.*

Christ died for the church

Christ's death is related not simply to individuals, but to the people of God, the church. The announcement to Mary about the impending birth of Jesus was that he would save *his people* from their sins.

It was clear, when Jesus took the cup and gave it to his disciples at the last supper, that he saw his death as bringing a new 'Israel' or people of God into being. Ever since that time, the church has remembered in the Lord's supper the cost Christ paid to found the church.

Christ builds the church

Jesus came to found, not a philosophy, but a community. It was basic to the early Christians' thought that new converts were immediately added to the fellowship; that all who had fellowship with the Father and the Son would be related to one another.

It was more than addition, however. Christ is the very source of the church's life, and so to be in the church is to experience Christ's life in a unique way. By his Spirit he directs the church, gives spiritual gifts to its members and creates unity and love.

Christ protects the church

In the Old Testament God's people were often protected by God, for example, in the story of the blazing furnace in the book of Daniel.

In the New Testament, we are told that Christ protects his people, the church. He defends the church from the attacks of Satan, and preserves it in

BIBLE CHECK

Died Matthew 1:21; 26:26-29   Acts 20:28
Builds Ephesians 4:11-16   Acts 2:46,47

adversity. More than this, he provides the power for the church to launch its own attacks against Satan. The church is not on the *defensive* – it is on the *offensive*.

Christ purifies the church

In the Old Testament, some of the prophets pictured Israel as a wife who had been unfaithful to her husband. God's people had been unfaithful to the promises they had made in their covenant with him.

The church is only seen as faithful and pure in the New Testament because of Christ. He has cleansed the church by his death, and continues to keep her holy. We are told that finally Christ will receive the church as a perfect bride, faithful and pure.

Christ intercedes for the church

The word 'intercede' means to act on someone else's behalf as a peacemaker. It is encouraging to know that because of Christ's death on our behalf, he is now in heaven as a man, representing us before the Father.

Because Christ intercedes for us, we are assured of at least three guarantees. First, we are forgiven because of his death. Second, we have free access to God because of his presence in heaven. Third, we are protected against condemnation for our sins by his words spoken in our defence.

Christ prepares for the church

Jesus reassured his friends when he warned them of his departure that they need not be anxious about the future, as he would be preparing a home for them. This shows us that Christ loves the church, and longs to enjoy the company of those who believe in him. His work will not be complete until the church is in the place he has prepared for it.

Postscript *Christ's love for his church led him to give up his own life for her. The church is called to do the same — to submit to the interests of her Lord and to fulfil his will.*

Protects Daniel 3:19-27 Matthew 16:18,19
Purifies Jeremiah 3:6,14 Ephesians 5:25-27
Intercedes Hebrews 7:25-27 1 John 2:1 Romans 8:34
Prepares John 14:1-4 1 Thessalonians 4:16,17

THOUGHT STARTERS

1 Consider the message of Revelation 3:1-6. John is conveying Christ's message to the church in Sardis (in present-day Turkey). How is this passage relevant to the church in general, and to your fellowship today? List the accusations, the challenges, and the promises of these verses.

2 'The Bible knows nothing of solitary religion' (John Wesley). Why should a Christian bother about the church of Jesus Christ?

3 Look at Revelation 1:5,6. What has Jesus Christ done for his church?

4 Read Daniel 3:13-28. What message is there in this story for today's church?

Tromso Cathedral, Norway. 'Christ loved the church and gave himself up for her' (Ephesians 5:25).

ITS AUTHORITY AND MISSION

The Key Truth *The church is not a passive society in the world. It receives its power and direction from Jesus Christ, who has given it his authority to fulfil his mission.*

Guarding the truth

The church is not to create truth, but guard it. It is described as the pillar of the truth; as contender for the faith that has been entrusted to God's people.

Thus the church must follow the apostles both in its standard of teaching and quality of mission. It must do more than guard the truth – it must proclaim it. Equally, it must do more than speak – it must speak the truth. The church is to be scripturally-minded and missionary-hearted.

Correcting the unruly

The Bible teaches that the authority of church leaders must be held in high regard if there is to be healthy discipline in the fellowship. On the other hand, leaders are to be held accountable for their standard of teaching and personal morality.

Indiscipline, immorality and division in the church are not to be condoned. However, all disciplinary measures are to be tempered by the desire to build up the offender and by the forgiveness that surrounds the family of Christ.

Challenging evil

Morally, spiritually and doctrinally, the church of God has always been surrounded by evil. The Bible teaches that evil can be overcome by the power of good. The church must challenge evil by its vigilance and by its determination to live and preach the truth.

BIBLE CHECK

Guarding 1 Timothy 3:15 Jude 3 1 Timothy 6:20
Correcting Hebrews 13:17 1 Corinthians 5:9-13

Evangelising the world

Before he ascended, Jesus gave his disciples a specific command that is to be obeyed by the church in every age. They were to make disciples everywhere, spreading the good news of Christ throughout the world.

We are to announce that Jesus Christ, once crucified for the sins of the world, is alive, and that he is Lord; that forgiveness and the gift of his Spirit are for all who belong to him through repentance and faith. The message is to be proclaimed universally, obediently, relevantly, joyfully and yet urgently. We do it at his command.

Serving the world

Jesus never expected the church to be a proclaimer of words without being a performer of deeds. Christian service is a partner of evangelism, both activities being a necessary part of the mission of God.

Christ is the example for the service that his church is commanded to bring to the world. He fed the hungry, he healed the sick and he brought hope to the despairing. He identified with humanity in all its needs. The same should be true of the fellowship he came to create.

Glorifying God

The church lives for the glory of God. In all that it does, it should direct attention and praise to God. It fulfils this purpose as it bears fruit in faithful service, and mirrors his love.

More particularly, it glorifies God as, following in the steps of Christ, it suffers with him. Jesus said that the hour of his death was the hour of greatest glory. So the suffering and the glory of God's kingdom are combined in Jesus.

Postscript *It is repeatedly in the very weakness of the church that its greatest power is seen.*

Challenging Romans 12:17-21 Jude 19-21
Evangelising Matthew 28:18-20 1 Thessalonians 1:5-10
Serving 1 John 3:17,18 Titus 3:8 Philippians 2:5-7
Glorifying John 12:27,28 1 Peter 4:12-14 Revelation 1:9

THOUGHT STARTERS

1 Read Acts 12:1-19. Consider the church's situation. What were its problems? Its mood? Its influence? Its surprises?

2 Where does the balance lie in practice, for you, between spreading the good news and giving practical service? What adjustments do you need to make?

3 How do you react to disagreements in your fellowship? How far do the words of 2 Timothy 2:23-26 apply?

4 To what extent are you able to take a positive initiative where you are, in being the 'salt' that improves society (Matthew 5:13)?

Cutting through rock, North Wales. 'We are God's fellow-workers' (1 Corinthians 3:9).

ITS ORDINANCES

The Key Truth *Baptism and the Lord's supper were both instituted by Jesus Christ as dynamic symbols of the gospel. The water of baptism signifies cleansing and entry into God's church. The bread and wine of the holy communion signify the receiving of Christ's body and blood, given for us in death.*

BAPTISM

Admission to membership
Ever since Christ's command to make disciples and to baptise them in the name of the Trinity, baptism with water has been the outward distinguishing mark of the Christian.

More than a symbol
When an Ethiopian official was baptised by Philip the evangelist, he was full of joy, although his knowledge of Jesus was limited. Baptism is a powerful event. Received rightly, it becomes a means of God's grace to the Christian.

Death to the old life
Baptism is a farewell to the old life – it is a baptism into the death of Christ. It signifies that the one baptised has been crucified with him, and that the life of sin and self belongs to the past.

Rising to the new life
Baptism is the emergence to the new life; it powerfully speaks to Christians of being raised with Christ, of walking in the light, of peace with God.

Identification with Christ
In his own .baptism, Jesus identified with sinful humanity. In our baptism we are privileged to identify with him, unashamed to be known by his name.

BIBLE CHECK

Admission Acts 2:41 **Symbol** Acts 8:38,39 **Death** Romans 6:3,4 · **Rising** Colossians 2:12 **Identification**

THE LORD'S SUPPER

We commemorate

Christ left us no monument or memorial; he never even wrote a book. What he left us was a fellowship 'meal' by which we could draw close to him and remember the sacrifice of his body and his blood, given for us in death. *This is the backward look.*

We communicate

It is not a dead Christ who is worshipped in the holy communion, but a risen Saviour. As his people share in the bread and wine, they give thanks and praise, and use the opportunity to renew their fellowship with the risen Lord. *This is the upward look.*

We appropriate

Jesus told his disciples to 'take' the bread, as he sat with them. Here is no one-man drama. We are not spectators, but deeply involved; if we come to the Lord's supper with a right attitude, we receive God's grace and strength for Christian living. *This is the inward look.*

We participate

The disciples all drank from the cup, as it was passed from one to another. It is, indeed, a sharing occasion. Believers do not come together in this way merely as individuals, but as a family. *This is the outward look.*

We anticipate

Christ told his disciples that the Lord's supper should be observed regularly – until his return. Then our communion with him will be direct, face to face. Thus the service is a pointer ahead. *This is the forward look.*

Postscript *It is important not to under-emphasise the value of these two ordinances, given by Jesus Christ. Through them we come to a deeper awareness of Christ's death and living presence.*

Galatians 3:27 **Commemorate** Luke 22:19,20 **Communicate** John 6:56 **Appropriate** Mark 14:22 **Participate** 1 Corinthians 10:16,17 **Anticipate** 1 Corinthians 11:26

THOUGHT STARTERS

1 Read Luke 22:14-27. Why did Jesus connect this event with the Old Testament Passover (see Exodus 12:25-27), and with the new covenant, prophesied by Jeremiah (Jeremiah 31:31-34)?

2 Read Acts 16:29-33. In these verses, baptism is shown to be an important event in the Christian's life. Why do you think that baptism is important?

3 As you attend the Lord's supper or holy communion, in what frame of mind should you come – towards Christ himself, yourself, and your neighbour?

4 Pick out the encouraging factors about that evening, and also the discouraging elements. What do they tell us about the gospel and ourselves?

Holly with berries. 'This cup is the new covenant in my blood; do this, whenever you drink it, in remembrance of me' (1 Corinthians 11:25).

ITS MINISTRY AND ORDER

The Key Truth *The church is to maintain a presence for God in the world, proclaiming his message and uplifting his name, under the guidance of appointed leaders.*

Preaching and teaching

The acceptance of Christianity's revealed truth has never been an optional extra in the church. We read in the New Testament of the standard or form of teaching required for growth and discipleship.

The issue of false teaching is dealt with on page after page of the New Testament letters. What protected the infant church was its anchorage in the apostolic teaching, received not merely on an intellectual level, but practised in daily life.

Prayer and intercession

Prayer was the power-house of the early church. It was the unseen weapon that established bridgeheads for the gospel in areas dominated by idolatry and moral darkness.

Prayer is the way in which God's power becomes effective, unhindered by considerations of space, time, culture, or even the prison bars erected by men.

Fellowship and caring

It has been pointed out that the early church was revolutionary. This was not because it roused slaves against their masters, but because it was more revolutionary still – it demolished the old distinctions altogether. The true liberation was freedom in Christ.

People divided by social status, religious background and language now became brothers and sisters in God's household. The apostles taught that widows are of importance in God's family; the sick are to be prayed for, and the hungry fed.

BIBLE CHECK

Preaching Romans 6:17   1 Timothy 1:3-7   Acts 2:42
Prayer Acts 4:31   Romans 15:30   1 Timothy 2:1,2

Worship and praise

Worship is the main purpose of the church. Jesus promised that even where only two or three met in his name, there he would be present with them. Praise and thanksgiving are the distinctive marks of a living church.

The worship of the Christian fellowship is not tied to a building or a structured order, although it is possible that 'liturgies' (forms of worship) were developing by the time the New Testament letters were written.

However the New Testament clearly states that it is not only the leaders who worship God, but all God's people. There is a 'priesthood of all believers', offering spiritual sacrifices.

Leadership and government

In the early church even the precise patterns and titles of ministry differed a little from church to church. Ephesus had 'elders', while Philippi had 'bishops' (both presumably describing the same function of pastoral oversight). There were also 'deacons' who served in a helping capacity, while the apostles were in a class of their own.

Those in the pastoral ministry belong to the church – the church does not belong to them. They are God's gift to the church. They are to feed the flock, they are to be blameless in their beliefs and in their conduct, and their ministry is to resemble that of Christ, who came to be a servant of all.

Postscript *It is important neither to create a hierarchy, through undue elevation of the leadership, nor to endanger truth and order in the church, through devaluation of those with oversight.*

Fellowship Colossians 3:11 1 Timothy 5:1,2 James 1:27
Worship Colossians 3:16 Hebrews 13:15,16 1 Peter 2:5,9
Leadership Philippians 1:1 1 Corinthians 3:5 Titus 1:5-9

THOUGHT STARTERS

1 Study 1 Peter 5:1-11. List the qualities to be found in one who shepherds God's flock. What was the association in Peter's mind that prompted these terms? Check your answer with John 21:15-17.

2 What are the tensions that the church of Christ inevitably experiences (verses 5-9)?

3 Look at 1 Timothy 4:11-16. These are Paul's words to a young church leader, Timothy. What are the responsibilities and rewards of church leadership? In what ways should we pray for our leaders?

4 Why is the church not a 'democracy'? And yet, why is it not a hierarchy?

Bernese Oberland, Switzerland. 'We have different gifts according to the grace given us' (Romans 12:6).

The Last Things

THE HOPE OF THE CHRISTIAN

The Key Truth   *The Christian's hope is a confidence in the rule and purposes of God, which find their goal in the return of Jesus Christ at the end of the age.*

The promises to God's people

God is working in history. The Christian is confident in the righteousness of God, which is working through the events of this world towards the final glory that must eventually follow the ministry and sufferings of Christ. It is his personal return that will usher in the new age.

Resting on the predictions of the Old Testament, the promises of Christ and the conviction of the apostles, the Christian is assured of the sovereign control of God to the end of time.

The fulfilment of God's purposes

The preaching of the apostles demonstrated the Christian belief that the return of Jesus, to make all things new, would be the ultimate fulfilment of his work of salvation.

For the believer, the appearance of Christ will come as the longed-for conclusion and perfection of the salvation already won through the sacrifice of the cross.

The defeat of God's enemies

The outcome of the conflict between good and evil is already settled. The death and subsequent resurrection of Jesus has ensured the defeat of sin, death, and all the powers of evil.

But it will not be until Christ's public and powerful return in glory that God's righteousness will be finally upheld. God's victory will then be evident to all.

BIBLE CHECK

Promise   1 Peter 1:10-12   Isaiah 11:1-9
Fulfilment   Acts 3:17-21   Romans 8:18-23

A living hope

It is Christ who fills the Christian with the confident expectation the Bible calls 'hope'. All the New Testament passages which describe the last things focus their attention on him.

It is in the resurrection of Jesus that we find particular encouragement. Our living hope is that like him we too shall rise from death to enjoy the new heaven and the new earth from which death and decay are banished. Christ's followers await a new body, incorruptible and powerful. This body will relate to the old existence, but Paul tells us that it will be significantly different.

A steadfast hope

The quality of Christian hope is that it imparts courage and patience for the present. It is not a vague desire for better times, nor is it a resigned and passive submission to life's problems while we wait for a new tomorrow.

The hope that is centred in Christ has kept the church through the ages during persecution and hardship. It is the hope that demolishes fear, and transforms pessimism into godly and practical optimism.

A purifying hope

Our hope in the return of Christ in the future should have a deep effect on the way we live now. Ours is not the hope of the curious who look only for the details of signs and dates while remaining detached and unaffected.

To the Christian, Christ's return is a reality. As a result, priorities, decisions and life-style will inevitably be shaped by the thought of his coming.

Postscript *Christian history indicates that those who have their eyes on the next life are the ones who are most effective in this.*

Defeat Philippians 2:9-11 1 Corinthians 15:24-26
Living 1 Peter 1:3-5 1 Corinthians 15:20-23, 51-55
Steadfast 1 Thessalonians 1:3 Romans 8:24,25
Purifying 1 John 3:2,3 Hebrews 10:23-25 Jude 24,25

THOUGHT STARTERS

1 Read 1 Peter 1:1-12. What were the circumstances of the readers of this letter? How can a Christian rejoice (verse 8) in the midst of adversity (verse 6)? What is the nature of the Christian hope, and how is it created?

2 Christians love someone they have never seen (1 Peter 1:8). How is such love generated and made a reality? Check your answer with Romans 15:4.

3 In what ways do you look forward to the future, and to what extent do you fear it?

4 How can the Christian's view of the future make a serious contribution to society as it attempts to grapple with the problems of tomorrow?

'We wait for the blessed hope – the glorious appearing of our great God and Saviour, Jesus Christ' (Titus 2:13).

THE PRELUDE TO CHRIST'S RETURN

The Key Truth *Before Christ returns, Christians may expect to see varying degrees of disorder in the world. This gives them an opportunity to evangelise and offer hope.*

BEFORE THE RETURN – DISORDER

In the natural realm

It is extremely important that as we read in the Bible about the famines, earthquakes and plagues that will feature before Christ's return, we should not be too quick to identify such an era with our own.

The Bible's repeated use of the phrase, 'the last times' refers to the entire period between Christ's first and second comings. Therefore, before Christ's return we should not be surprised to see natural and even cosmic disasters.

In the social realm

Stress and social disorder are characteristics of the period before Christ's second coming. We are told that people will be arrogant and proud, materialistic and immoral. The Bible says that these will be terrible times when human sin is unchecked.

There will also be those who make a mockery of religion and of any talk of a return by Jesus Christ.

In the international realm

Jesus made it plain, as he taught his disciples, that wars, revolutions and political disturbances would characterise the coming age. These events would not mean that the end had come – they would be signs of the presence and advance of the kingdom. They would be the labour pains heralding the birth of the new order.

BIBLE CHECK

Natural Luke 21:11,25 Romans 8:22
Social 2 Timothy 3:1-5 Jude 18 2 Peter 3:3,4

In the family realm

Hatred and division, even within families, were predicted by Jesus Christ as being features of the last times.

The family relationship would be endangered, and loyalties would be strained – in certain circumstances to the point of betrayal.

In the personal realm

During the last times, those who have no relationship with God will experience an increase in fear and insecurity.

Jesus predicted that the situation would be similar to that of Noah's generation. There would be aimlessness, with men and women eating and drinking, getting married and going about their daily business – yet estranged from God and with no real purpose for living.

In the spiritual realm

From descriptions in the Book of Revelation we can see that the spiritual realm will be unrestricted in its rebellion. Paul describes the coming of 'the man of lawlessness', who will declare himself to be God, and will demand worship. Also there will be numerous 'false christs' who will attempt to lead people away from the truth.

The church, while exercising great influence through its proclamation of the gospel, will nevertheless face considerable pressure and persecution during the last times.

Postscript *In the Gospels, Jesus' prediction of the destruction of the Jerusalem Temple merges with his description of the last times. Whatever our interpretation, Christ's prediction about the Temple is a prefigure of his further prediction of the end.*

International Mark 13:7,8 Luke 21:9,10
Family Mark 13:12 Matthew 10:34-36
Personal Luke 21:26 Matthew 24:37-39
Spiritual Matthew 24:4-14 2 Thessalonians 2:3-10

THOUGHT STARTERS

1 Read Matthew 24:3-14. Try to list the events and patterns foreseen by the Lord as taking place between his departure from earth and his return. In what way do you think they apply to this generation?

2 Why was Jesus not more specific? Compare your findings with Matthew 12:38-42 and Matthew 24:36.

3 Reflect on the attitude that we should have regarding Jesus' warnings of world events. How should his words affect our lives today?

4 What is faulty in the desire to know the precise details about the Lord's coming? Compare your answer to Matthew 24:42 and Deuteronomy 29:29.

Chicago, USA. 'The creation itself will be liberated from its bondage . . .' (Romans 8:21).

THE RETURN OF CHRIST

The Key Truth *All Christians look forward to the personal return of Christ at the end of the age, as predicted by the Bible.*

CHRIST WILL RETURN

Prophetically
There are numerous Old Testament passages that refer to the kingly rule of Christ – predictions that plainly will not be fulfilled until his return.

The New Testament prophecies are found throughout the Gospels, Acts, the letters and the book of Revelation. They refer to Christ's return as a *Coming,* as a *Revealing,* as the *Day of the Lord* and as his *Appearing.*

Personally
We are not, of course, to think of Jesus as absent from the world and from his people at the present time, for he promised to be with his followers until the end.

But while he is with the church invisibly at present, by his Spirit, Christ's coming at the end will be visible and personal. The assurance was given to the apostles, at the time of the ascension, that it would be the very same Jesus who returned.

Visibly
The return of Jesus Christ will be no secret, hidden affair. The Bible teaches that earth's entire population will see the event.

To some, the appearing of Jesus will be a glorious and wonderful sight, but we also learn from the scriptures that many will be dismayed.

BIBLE CHECK

Prophetically Daniel 7:13,14   1 Thessalonians 4:16-18
Personally Matthew 28:20   Acts 1:11

Suddenly

The Lord spoke of life in this world at the time of his coming as being very similar to life in Noah's day at the time of the flood. Marriage, eating and drinking – life would be continuing as usual.

But then, at a single stroke, everything would be interrupted. The Bible describes Jesus Christ's return as being like a lightning flash, like a thief in the night and like a master paying an unexpected visit on his servants. It is clear that people will be taken unawares, in spite of the many warnings of scripture. All Jesus' parables relating to his coming include this aspect of suddenness.

Triumphantly

This second coming of Christ will be utterly different from the squalid obscurity in which he first came. The return will be accompanied by great power and splendour. In the face of the victorious majesty and power of Jesus Christ's appearing, every person will be forced to acknowledge that he is truly Lord.

Conclusively

The appearing of Jesus Christ will be the final chapter in the human story. His coming will bring governments, nations, authorities and every kind of enemy of God under his rule and judgement.

Death will be destroyed. Satan, and the whole empire of evil will be overthrown for ever. And Christ's people will be united to their Lord in the home that he has prepared for them.

Postscript   *History is full of examples of false predictions relating to the time of Christ's return. The Christian is best prepared for this event by being involved in active, obedient service.*

Visibly Matthew 24:30   Revelation 1:7
Suddenly Matthew 24:27,36-51   1 Thessalonians 5:2,3
Triumphantly Luke 21:27,28   Philippians 2:9-11
Conclusively 1 Corinthians 15:24   1 Thessalonians 4:17

THOUGHT STARTERS

1 Study 1 Thessalonians 4:13-5:11. Why was this passage written? From these words, how may we understand the coming of Christ, in relation to Christians who have died, the Day itself, its timing and our right preparation for it?

2 Compare John 14:3 with 1 Thessalonians 4:16-18. How does Paul's teaching relate to Christ's?

3 What should be your attitude to readers of the Bible who, while believing in the main fact of Christ's coming, may not agree with you on every point of interpretation?

4 What do non-Christian friends of yours think about the future of the world? How does their view differ from yours?

Sun-dial at Fort Belan, North Wales. 'No one knows about that day or hour . . . but only the Father' (Mark 13:32).

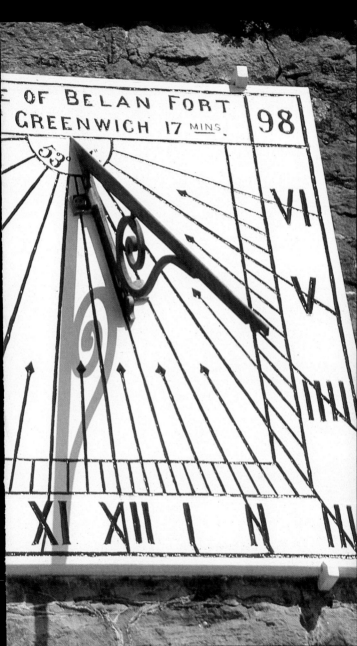

THE JUDGEMENT

The Key Truth   *The final judgement will be the climax of this world's events. It will set right the injustices of history, underline the choices of individuals, and demon-strate the righteousness of God and the victory of Jesus Christ.*

God will be declared as just

The final judgement is a definite future event that will take place at the second coming of Christ. The Bible says that it is unavoidable – as unavoidable as death itself.

At the judgement the balances of true justice will be set right for ever. There will be no excuse left to any who come under judgement – for it will be seen by everybody that the dealings of God are completely just and righteous.

Christ will be acknowledged as Lord

The judgement will signify the end of world history and the struggle between good and evil. Every power that has stood in opposition to God will be put under Christ's feet, and every tongue will confess that he is Lord.

At the judgement, Jesus Christ will receive the glory and worship that is due to him from his people, for he will have gathered them to himself from the whole earth. Their sins will not be counted against them, for by his death on the cross he has already taken their judgement upon himself.

Christians will be accountable for their service

While no Christian will be judged on the basis of the sins he has committed, it is taught in the Bible that

---

BIBLE CHECK

God   Hebrews 9:27   Psalm 96:13   Acts 17:31
Christ   1 Corinthians 15:24-26   John 5:24   Philippians 2:11

Christ's people will be assessed for the quality of their service.

No Christian will ever be lost, but the coming Day will expose our work, which will be rewarded according to its worth. The faithful Christian is thus challenged to please his returning master throughout life's present opportunity.

The disobedient will be rejected for their unbelief

The basis of the judgement will be the response that individuals have made to the light that God has given them. The great sin of the New Testament consists in rejecting the light of Christ. When asked what *the* vital priority of life was, Jesus replied that it was to believe in himself.

The separation from God to which unbelievers are condemned is therefore no more than an underlining of their own choices regarding God's revelation to them.

Satan will be destroyed for ever

Satan is not all-powerful. The book of Revelation shows that he is very active in many different ways, but he does not occupy the centre – for God never leaves his throne.

Thus, the judgement will bring the victory of the cross to completion. Satan and his allies will be overthrown and destroyed by God.

Postscript *Judgement is not a popular theme in societies which have become soft and indulgent. However, we must recognise that by the choices individuals make, they sentence themselves.*

Christians Romans 14:12 2 Corinthians 5:9,10
1 Corinthians 3:10-15
Disobedient John 3:19; 6:28,29 2 Thessalonians 1:7-9
Satan Revelation 20:10

THOUGHT STARTERS

1 Read Matthew 25:1-13. What is the main thrust of this parable of Jesus? Contrast the two groups of girls. What does this passage teach us about the end times, and about our choices in life?

2 At the end, there will be a separation between evil and good. Is the world getting better or worse? Compare your thoughts with Matthew 13:24-30.

3 What does 1 Corinthians 3:12-15 teach Christian people about their responsibilities and opportunities?

4 What does Christ's teaching about judgement tell us about the nature of man himself?

Solidified volcanic lava, Hawaii. 'Man is destined to die once, and after that to face judgement' (Hebrews 9:27).

THE RESURRECTION

The Key Truth *The Bible teaches that Christians will be raised from death to enjoy eternal life with God.*

Christ its guarantee

Christianity presents the resurrection of the body as the final goal of our salvation – a supernatural event coinciding with the return of Jesus Christ.

This resurrection, which is the inheritance of every Christian, derives its pattern from Christ. The Bible says that Christ's resurrection is like the first sheaf of a large harvest, in which all Christians will be gathered. This is what the Bible means when it uses the word 'firstfruits'. Christ's resurrection is the guarantee of this event.

Nature its illustration

This expectation of a bodily resurrection is illustrated by Paul in his first letter to the Christians in Corinth.

Paul answers the objection that the resurrection is impossible, by referring to the miracle of sowing and reaping, in which a small seed is transformed into a plant. The resurrection does not mean a mere shadowy existence of the soul, but a glorious and transformed body.

Eternal life its outcome

The resurrection body is designed for a totally different environment than that of our earthly existence. When it is raised, it is a spiritual body, suited for life in the presence of God. There, believers will know an existence unlimited by the effects of the fall.

BIBLE CHECK

Christ 1 Corinthians 15:20-23   Philippians 3:20,21
Nature 1 Corinthians 15:35-38

From humiliation to glory

Christians are assured in the Bible that when they finally see Christ, they will have a body like his. We are not given many details about the nature of the resurrection body, beyond that the believer's body is weak and ugly at death, but that when raised, it possesses marvellous beauty and strength.

Probably, the reason why we are only given a limited understanding of the resurrection body is that in this new life the focus will be on Christ himself and not on the details of secondary importance. He will be at the centre, and that is what really matters.

From the natural to the spiritual

At death, the believer's body is physical; at the resurrection it is spiritual. If Christ's resurrection body is the pattern, then we can understand that this body will have unusual powers.

It will be a body that has continuity with the old body (and the indication is that there will be recognition in the next life), and yet a body suited to a totally different dimension.

From mortality to immortality

All reminders of death, decay and disease will be banished from the new bodies of Christ's people. The apostle Paul seems to indicate that those believers who have died before Christ's return still await their resurrection bodies and for the present are without a body, although truly with Christ. They, like those who are still alive at Christ's return, will be raised to live for ever.

Postscript *The Christian's hope is not to escape from the body, but to be raised as a new body to live the quality of life God has always intended for us.*

Eternal Life 1 Thessalonians 4:16,17 John 5:24-26; 6:40
Glory 1 Corinthians 15:43 1 John 3:2
Spiritual John 20:19 1 Corinthians 15:44 Luke 24:36-43
Immortality 1 Corinthians 15:42,50-55 Philippians 1:21-24

THOUGHT STARTERS

1 Read 1 Corinthians 15:20-28. How does Christ's resurrection affect the future? In what sense do we understand the defeat of death? How is this confidence reflected in Christian living today?

2 What difference, in practice, does a Christian faith seem to make to people in the face of death?

3 Turn to the Old Testament passage of Ezekiel 37:1-14, which relates to the message of resurrection. Think and pray about situations that need this kind of transformation.

4 Because Christ is risen, we too shall be raised from death. In what ways does this give the Easter story extra meaning for you?

Cherry blossom, U.S.A.
'The dead will be raised imperishable, and we will be changed'
(1 Corinthians 15:52).